WARNER BERTHOFF is Professor of English at Harvard University and author of several books, including *The Ferment of Realism, 1884-1919* (1965).

ALSO IN NORTON PAPERBOUND EDITIONS

The Confidence-Man: His Masquerade by Herman Melville (*a Norton Critical Edition, edited by Hershel Parker*)

Moby-Dick by Herman Melville (a Norton Critical Edition, edited by Harrison Hayford and Hershel Parker)

Moby-Dick as Doubloon: Essays and Extracts (1851-1970) edited by Hershel Parker and Harrison Hayford

THE EXAMPLE OF
MELVILLE

BY WARNER BERTHOFF

The Norton Library
W · W · NORTON & COMPANY · INC ·
NEW YORK

TO

LAURENCE STAPLETON

AND

RICHMOND LATTIMORE

Whose every work, of thy most early wit,
Came forth example and remains so yet.

First published in the Norton Library 1972
by arrangement with the Princeton University Press

Books That Live
The Norton imprint on a book means that in the publisher's estimation it is a book not for a single season but for the years.
W. W. Norton & Company, Inc.

SBN 393 00595 X

PRINTED IN THE UNITED STATES OF AMERICA

1 2 3 4 5 6 7 8 9 0

CONTENTS

THE EXAMPLE OF MELVILLE

"Nor book, nor author of the book, hath any sequel, though each hath its last lettering."—*Pierre,* XXVI, *vi*

INTRODUCTION

MELVILLE: A PROBLEM

". . . a dark little black-letter volume in golden clasps, entitled 'Hawthorne: A Problem.' "—MELVILLE TO HAWTHORNE, April 1851

THE CONCERN of this book is with the example Melville presents as a writer, as it still lies before us in his work. The scope of what I have to say, therefore, is both comprehensive and restricted. My emphasis is not, except incidentally, upon those various particular aspects of subject, theme, and personal outlook that reveal themselves in Melville's successive books and in the few letters and journals that survive. These are the topics a voluminous criticism and scholarship have, with one stress or another, rewardingly pursued during the forty-odd years since his recovery, around 1920, as a major author: the character and personal history of the man, the phases of his thought, the general import of his characteristic ideas and preoccupations, the meaning of his remarkable public career, the meaning of this or that individual work. But it is first of all as a writer, a master of expression, that Melville remains with us, not as a philosopher, nor as a phenomenon of intellectual and cultural history, nor even—however much one is wanted—as a provider of "scripture." It is of course a perfectly objective tribute to Melville's work that it should so forcibly attract this other kind of concern, and seem to lend itself to speculative interpretation. Moreover, the kinds of judgment that result may have much to suggest about certain actual properties and conditions of his achievement. At the same time—and this is my present point of departure—it has somehow remained possible for an informed reviewer to contend that we have not yet got an "adequate general account of Melville" [1]—which is to say, of the kind of writer he was and of the species of performance which he presents us with at his best.

For what would we really know the meaning of? We read for what we find—for entertainment; for edification of our leisure; for the thought, insight, information, testimony, display of action and character, and all the impressions of life which according to the accident of his choice and of his habit and competence a writer may give us; for the charm, wit, force and logic of feeling, and felicity and accuracy of his rendering. We read for the matter, as the manner persuades us (and our readiness allows). In presuming to report on our reading, in the special practice of criticism, the first job, as T. S. Eliot once put it, is "elucidation and the correction of taste"—which means pointing up what is there to be appreciated, according to the whole nature of the work in question, and opposing such misconceptions as periodically grow up in the way of a fair enjoyment. Very properly, good criticism is piecemeal. It works at details and along tangents, and sets its course of argument according to the obstructions peculiar to the time and occasion. It must despair of total demonstration; with questions of meaning and value it can scarcely hope to prove what the ordinary observant reader may not find out for himself, though it can (and this justifies it) encourage him to look again, to see more discriminatingly, to trust and to hold to what he has found. Like any writing or art, criticism is a communication according to the nature of its primary objects as well as of its own argumentative ends.

In some instances, however, as with that writer whose work so impresses us that we set out to absorb ourselves systematically in the whole of it, the focus of our attention may change

[1] *Times Literary Supplement*, December 30, 1955, review of Edward H. Rosenberry, *Melville and the Comic Spirit*.

somewhat, for what seems worth elucidating may lie a little deeper than any single aspect of his accomplishment can show. The particulars of the work itself—themes, ideas, procedures, forms—come to seem to a degree incidental. We grow aware of something further, of a continuous imaginative presence and energy sustaining these particulars and positively generating them, of a distinct and original signature suggestive of some whole new apprehension, and corresponding organization, of things. When this kind of impression emerges, the designations and categories criticism usually relies on may strike us as not quite to the point. To be told, for example (to borrow some characteristic findings of Melville criticism in recent years), that the writer we thus respond to is best described as a "naturalist" or perhaps as a "Manichaean," or that he belongs to the "party of irony" or represents "Stoic acceptance," or that he is significant in possessing "the symbolic imagination" or perhaps the sense of "blackness," or that he was one who intuited transcendental "polarities" but "never developed a firm novelistic or poetic sense of things," is at a certain point to be put off from what really interests us. This is the language of the Age of Names, as Proust called it; and "the magnificence of names," so Melville himself wrote in *Pierre*, "must not mislead us as to the humility of things." Such names are probably useful in their way (but how much of our criticism is mere gossip and name-dropping). What they point to in a writer's work, however, are certain contingent attitudes, certain *ad hoc* postures of thought and feeling, which may indeed serve to place it as a body of expression in the stream of general history but which are not the true locus of its special virtue and power. It is not this normal attitudinizing (the staple of sub-literature, as of common taste and opinion) that commands the kind of attention we are compelled to give the great writer—beyond such attention as we might decently give the life, the career, the personal bias and feeling, of any documented human creature.

Rather it is that inward and continuous activity of outgoing imagination in him which puts its defining stamp (perhaps not always distinctly) on everything he sets his hand to.

This imaginative force, this tangible creativity of expression, we recognize in two practical ways: first, by its achievement of *style*, its power to re-establish the common language it is bound to as the very sign and prime agent of our common civil existence; and then, by its achievement of *form*, its power to render the saleable genres and conventions of mere literature, including those of its own devising, plastic once again to our life's profoundest impulses. This double power is what we come to value in literature, and only secondarily (though then for a time overwhelmingly) the particular objects it produces. For it tells of a vital ground of possibility in life which is somehow accessible to practical understanding, and which thus remains to be tapped anew—by just such particular acts of response and control, and by that free release of disciplined and concerted energy, along the live circuits of the common consciousness, which is the nerve and pulse of original art. "The clearest, most memorable and important fact about art," Pasternak said, "is its conception, and the world's best creations, those which tell of the most diverse things, in reality describe their own birth." [2]

For is it not with the writer as it is with ourselves? We pass through our experience and grow into the inclinations, habits, ideas, convictions, custom, and style of behavior that identify us as individuals. And simultaneously we grow interested in all these things and in their prevailing, their turning out true to some approving general order of being; we begin willy-nilly to seek, on whatever scale, to pursue and extend them. They are the earnest of our actual existence, the legacy of our phenomenal continuance as human beings. Yet in a fundamental sense these things are accidental, and therefore chiefly of conversational, not to say statistical, interest. They are the result

[2] *Safe Conduct*, II, vii, tr. Beatrice Scott.

of all the contingencies that go to determine the course of our lives, that govern our unique natural histories. But how we deliver ourselves of these "mere contingent things, and things we know not," as Melville called them, is the distinguishing free variable; and this is not altogether accidental but in our keeping, and a true object of our most profoundly discriminating curiosity. Here or nowhere is the life, the being, we make for ourselves, and the place in which we know ourselves to be tried out, the writer in his effort along with the rest of us in ours.

II

A certain prodigality and force of imagination are more or less constant in Melville's performance as a writer. In the mass of his work, however, these qualities are no more a guarantee of formal control than mere force of personality can ever be of creative intelligence. And it is chiefly as a personality that Melville has been felt and rendered back to us by his more perceptive admirers—as if to illustrate his own notion that a writer's work is most meaningfully construed as an autobiographical cypher screening some otherwise unutterable personal testimony. The more useful contributions of scholarship have been those concerned principally with his personal presence and outlook, notably the documentary compilations of Jay Leyda and Eleanor Melville Metcalf, D. H. Lawrence's famous studies, and the variously conceived biographies of Raymond Weaver (it was after all the first) and John Freeman, and of Newton Arvin and Leon Howard.[3]

But we must allow that the actual person is unrecoverable, however vivid or intimate our impression of him. Even the course of his imaginative development is only very roughly and

[3] Good criticism of Melville's resources as an artist and of the formal properties of his work has been rarer. The valuable studies, I think, have been by Constance Rourke, F. O. Matthiessen, Charles Olson, and, again, Newton Arvin. Interpretations of themes and meanings in Melville's books, on the other hand, have been legion, but constitute more of a case study in contemporary intellectual folkways than an aid to understanding.

intermittently traceable. What *can* be known, what can be recovered and made use of, is what the common reader can know: the work itself, the specific product that the man's life and career brought forth and continue to be known for. This is the stuff of the example that comes down to us—and what more *should* we know who approach it in readiness and unconstraint, in the willing exertion of whatever faculties of response we are capable of? More data will doubtless be brought to light, facts of biography and background, information about the taste and fashion of the times, even new manuscripts or letters; natural curiosity will see to that, and will relish the findings. But such discoveries will only corroborate the conception we already have of Herman Melville. They are not likely to change it in any important way. They cannot even verify it, really, for our sense of what they signify will be drawn from the very qualities in the published writing which sent us in search of them. What interest would we take even in Melville's extraordinary letters of 1849–1852 if there were no such book as *Moby-Dick?*

Melville's strongly personal appeal as a writer is of a piece (scarcely less than Whitman's, though less calculatingly) with the actual progress of his career. It is a main part of our impression of him that we should find him manfully absorbed, at the moment of writing his books, in the activity and astonishing development of his own mind, yet peculiarly without personal presumption in the matter. The rough material for his first six books, everyone knows, came from his experiences at sea and in the Pacific islands. But once past the adventure-peddling of *Typee* and *Omoo*, his decisive inspiration as a writer was in this consuming inward growth. This, clearly, was the center and sum of his experience during the half-dozen years that culminated in *Moby-Dick* and *Pierre*. And it was a phenomenon of experience which pressed upon him as strongly and which he was able to exploit as graphically as the picturesque events of his earlier life before the mast and on the Polynesian beaches.

I want to make this point about Melville's growth as emphatically as possible, for it seems to me central to an accurate understanding of the shape of his career. The event that effectively opened the larger world of human action and sentiment to him as a writer, including the random world of his own youthful adventuring, was the rapid inward unfolding and expansion, in the years between *Typee* and *Moby-Dick,* of his own mind. It is not just that this event increased his personal resources or gave him a surer private measure of emotional truth and intellectual seriousness. More significantly, it gave him an intense and yet objective personal experience of one of the great creative conceptions of his era—by which I mean the conception of the "growth of the mind," as the earlier nineteenth century understood that phrase. This conception, rooted of course in the confident psychological inquiries of the Enlightenment, but thereafter enlivened by a new, quasi-religious attentiveness to all the irrational variety of the natural data, is perhaps the major original theme of Romantic thought and literature. It underlies, as a kind of formative analogy, one after another of the characteristic philosophical developments of the era—the individualism, the sense of evolutionary process, the historicism and vitalism, the various new organic concepts of existence and behavior that still shape the modern intelligence in every field of speculation—and serves moreover as a prime motive, in a moral sense, to their investigation. As the human mind grows, so all existence unfolds its secret logic. And by the accidents and timing of his own inward growth Melville found himself ready to take this great theme in charge. He found himself able, that is, to lodge his crowding private intuitions in a scheme of apprehension which was authoritatively established in his era's literature and yet far from being played out. As a result he could capitalize immediately and extravagantly upon certain major conventions for dealing with it—those conventions of understanding and expression that his pell-mell assimilation of Goethe, Emerson, Hawthorne, Coleridge, and Carlyle, among the masters of this theme in his century, had disclosed to him—without losing his own identity or direction.

There is not room in these pages for an adequate account of the idea of the "growth of the mind," with its double implication of development both in nature and in culture, and of its importance for Romantic literature in general. It had its origins in the whole broad complex of historical circumstances, including the revolutions in science and philosophy, that distinguishes the "modern" era. We may say this much, though, that it profoundly reflects the widening liberalizations of western society during and after the Enlightenment and the bourgeois revolution. As the system of social liberty advanced, an intuition of the moral and intellectual freedom of the human creature grew correspondingly—post-Kantian idealism provided an appropriate epistemology, and indicated a metaphysic—and an investigation (at once rationalist and scientific) of the natural conditions of this freedom is perhaps the central and determinative activity of philosophy and literature in the eighteenth and early nineteenth centuries. The theme seems also a characteristic product of the progressive loosening of Christian belief, and of the transferring of expectations as to the meaning and end of human life from the sanctions of theology to those of psychology and natural history.[4]

The writing which this conception organizes needs to be distinguished, however, from the innumerable accounts of spiritual conversion (or de-conversion) that fill up nineteenth-century literature, in which description of the process of the mind's changes is constrained to some doctrine of their appointed outcome and subordinated therefore to some given system of belief or intellectual allegiance. The interest in such accounts of how one kind of intensely conditioned behavior was shaken off

[4] For this reason, what Melville in *Billy Budd* cited as the lexicon of Christian understanding remains central to nearly every new nineteenth-century effort at philosophic reconstruction, especially in ethics and morals, and to a good many since. But not all who have gone on using this lexicon have had the wit and courtesy, as Melville did, to apologize for it.

and exchanged for another is a narrower interest finally, although the form they take may be masterly; whether the vehicle is an *Apologia Pro Sua Vita*, an *Autobiography of Mark Rutherford*, or a *Portrait of the Artist as a Young Man*, the display of "growth" is as circumscribed as in a Bunyan's *Grace Abounding*. What we feel at once in Melville's case is the absence of any such intense preliminary conditioning (the life of his psyche, as the third child of Maria Gansevoort and Allan Melville, in the New York of the 1820's and 1830's, is another matter). As a young man he seems underaffected; his father's description of him in childhood as being "of a docile & amiable disposition," intellectually tractable but without conspicuous motivation, carries weight, if only for lack of contrary evidence. And we may imagine that when his inward growth of mind began in earnest, he had nothing much in the way of settled conviction or bias to shake off—but for the same reason there was no conceivable end to the process. There would be no "belief," matching some positive indoctrination he had put behind him, that he could ever rest in, as Hawthorne was shrewdly to understand at their last extended meeting. His own deepest apprehension told him as much; it is characteristic that he should express his immediate consciousness of this whole consuming experience most directly in the form of a question—"Lord, when shall we be done growing?" [5]—and that at the close of *Mardi*, his first attempt to exploit this experience as a subject, he should leave us with the image of a heroic but frustrated seeker, pursued and pursuing, advancing alone over an "endless" sea.

III

The earliest readers of *Typee* (1846) and *Omoo* (1847) sensed, beyond the curiosity interest of the Polynesian materials, an ingratiating verve and facility of expression which were never altogether to desert Melville. John Murray, his first

[5] Letter to Hawthorne, November 1851.

publisher, suspected after reading him in manuscript that "Herman Melville" was the disguise of some "practiced writer." [6] Washington Irving, hearing passages from *Typee* read in proof, remarked on the "graphic" picturesqueness of the style. Fluency (an "American fluency," one English reviewer called it); a geniality only occasionally lapsing into archness; picturesqueness and abundance of descriptive detail—these helped to win Melville his quick popular success. It was left to Hawthorne, as discerning a reader as Melville has ever had, to put into words the something further that carries the promise, we now see, of the extraordinary career soon to follow, when he stressed the author's "freedom of view," arguing that it was this which gave Melville a necessary natural tolerance of his exotic materials and therefore made his book "wholesome" despite its undisguised voluptuousness.

This freedom of view was also, patently, a freedom of handling; there were legitimate doubts in 1846 and 1847 about the authenticity of Melville's chronicles of adventure. With *Mardi* (written during 1847–1848) it became a still broader and more strenuous freedom, opening out thirty-odd chapters along into the ambitious extravaganza of an allegorical voyage with the whole constituted world as its province. The rush of this ambitiousness—stylistic, philosophical, satiric, indiscriminately universal—outran Melville's technical competence, overtaxing the natural sense of pace and proportion in narrative which he had shown in the casually assembled but shaped and ordered chapters of *Typee* and *Omoo*. Yet there are signs in the latter stages of *Mardi* that he was catching up with himself. The book suffers to the last page from what one reviewer fairly described as "a continual straining after effect, an effort constantly at fine writing, a sacrifice of natural ease to artificial witticism," and more generally from what another called "the

[6] Biographical data is drawn, except as otherwise noted, from Jay Leyda, *The Melville Log* (New York, 1951), and Eleanor Melville Metcalf, *Herman Melville, Cycle and Epicycle* (Cambridge, Massachusetts, 1953).

apparent want of motive in the composition"; yet, as toward the end its focus becomes more directly subjective and the almost abandoned theme of the narrator-hero's private quest is strongly resumed, the writing is steadied by a counterbalancing gravity of tone and definiteness of notation. It is as though Melville had to grow accustomed—and could do it best by working ahead at top speed—not only to the new thoughts, the speculative insights and mysteries, which were crowding into his head, but also to the unforeseen and wholly intoxicating freedom of being a writer and having a story to tell.

He quickly came to know that *Mardi* was a failure, and as quickly wrote it off as a casualty of his mind's growth. Not three weeks after publication he told Evert Duyckinck that it seemed far back in the past to him, so rapidly did he feel his mood changing and his inward career hurrying him along. So powerfully did new conceptions of the kind of book he wanted to be known for, and the kind of truths he wanted to deliver, rise before him that he grudged the effort put into "beggarly" *Redburn* and *White-Jacket* in the spring and summer of 1849. But most readers now agree with what most reviewers remarked at the time, that these books (each was written in about six weeks) were better than anything he had yet done. And they were better in ways, we now see, that point to the special virtues of the greater work yet to come—*Redburn,* more coherent and sustained as narrative and richer in intimations of fundamental human character; *White-Jacket,* more robustly expansive and matter-of-factly panoramic in its free-and-easy, round-the-world, man-of-war setting. In both of these essentially documentary books, the writing, as Hawthorne remarked to Duyckinck, thrusts "unflinchingly" close to solid reality; yet both also strongly foreshadow the imaginative freedom and spaciousness of *Moby-Dick.*

With *Moby-Dick,* written during 1850 and 1851, much that is excitingly predicated in the earlier narratives is splendidly fulfilled—the metaphor of the ship as a world which was announced in the subtitle of *White-Jacket*, the world-spanning prospect of *Mardi*, the intuitions of general human nature and conduct which underscore *Redburn*. Melville's greatest chronicle is also, in plot and in moral scope, a remarkably successful assimilation, though hardly flawless, of the grand manner of poetic tragedy. Yet it is the scale and the setting as much as the form and argument of Ahab's drama that hold us to it; certainly Ishmael's meditative narration, and the epic celebration of the world-wide and universe-deep business of going whaling, are what make up the solid core of the book's greatness. The sphere of action in *Moby-Dick* is far more richly set out and furnished than in *Typee* or *Mardi*—but the decisive increment is not a matter of new themes or "metaphysical" insights, as might be assumed; it is a matter of an extraordinary further advance into observable fact and practical detail. Seemingly the whole thronged phenomenal world of actual human life and enterprise has been brought actively and expressly into view. Though all is finally conceived under the aspect of certain "heartless, ever-juvenile eternities," or of those conditions of life which are by nature indifferent to the human measure, both Ishmael's spirited ruminations and Ahab's intense soliloquies abound in references to the constituted and familiar nature of "this world." "This world"—the phrase rings through the book, and is an important clue, I think, to Melville's astonishing achievement of the epic grandeur he aimed for. The widening awarenesses which mark the growth of his mind have crystallized in *Moby-Dick* into a vivid and comprehensive conception of the given world and how it goes, and of the varieties of life it naturally harbors—as well as of what forces may ultimately preside over it.

But he was not done "growing" and "changing"—so he told Hawthorne with a kind of baffled awe the month *Moby-Dick* was published. He plunged on to write *Pierre*, V. S. Pritchett has remarked, "on one of those waves of hysterical exhaustion that are among the calamities of authorship." It is a bad book distinguished by passages of admirably original and exact writing. As Melville's one full exercise in the popular conventions of romantic melodrama, it represents, so the reviewer for *Graham's Magazine* declared, "a provoking perversion of talent and waste of power." But the same reviewer also found it superior "in force and subtlety of thinking and unity of purpose" to any of Melville's earlier books; and insofar as *Pierre* follows a shift of interest already apparent in the Ahab-dominated chapters at the end of *Moby-Dick,* turning inward from the constitution of "this world" to the natural life-process of the individual soul, we may well feel that it goes even more radically into certain conceptual sources of its inspiration than was the case even with *Moby-Dick.*

Pierre is clearly a turning point in Melville's career—his last prose work on a grand scale, his last free yielding to that rush of interior development which served him for education. Its hectic plot of overreaching and self-destruction looms now as a forecast of his own later retreat into virtual seclusion and anonymity. Yet for a time the volume of his work scarcely lessened. With a series of "magazinish" pieces for *Putnam's* and *Harper's* he again enjoyed, for three or four years more, a degree of the public acceptance and salability he had achieved with his first books. It is remarkable, however, that in this later work we find him making fewer concessions to popular taste than in the opening phase of his career. The best of it—"Bartleby the Scrivener," "Cock-a-Doodle-Doo!" "The Encantadas," parts of *Israel Potter,* "Benito Cereno," "Jimmy Rose," and "I and My Chimney" (all 1853–1856)—is as original in conception as *Moby-Dick,* though on a reduced scale, and as expert in performance as *Pierre* is confused and maladroit. It was Melville's strength and temper, and not his art, that finally gave way. All through the early and middle 1850's there were symptoms of depression and overwork which caused his family no little concern. As he labored at a new novel in 1856, he was felt to be running the risk of some really serious breakdown. In the fall of that year, with *The Confidence-Man* in the hands of a publisher, he set out on what was to be a long European tour of recuperation. It turned out instead to be the beginning of a permanent withdrawal. Thereafter he was to publish no more novels or magazine pieces.[7] Scarcely ten years after it had accidentally begun, the public career of this most gifted of American prose writers was over.

Subsequently he meditated, and marked the philosophical books he was reading, and wrote poems and a few related prose sketches and then one last sustained prose narrative. The poetry—of which the verse-record of certain Civil War events that he published as *Battle-Pieces* (1866) and the philosophical romance *Clarel* (1876) are most notable—shows little enough of technical facility, or what Hopkins called the "common teachable element" of rhetoric and prosody; for Melville turned to verse too late in his career and without anything like that apprenticeship to several varieties of masterly prose that underlies his earlier writing. But here and there it does show some of the qualities of the greatest poetry—particularly in its strong emotional control and intellectual energy (students of Melville's thought will always find it absorbing), and in the nervous expressive power with which now and again it lifts itself to its most intense concerns. It becomes on these occasions a perfect instance of what Hopkins described as the "Olympian" mode—"the language of strange masculine genius which suddenly, as it were, forces its way into the domain of poetry, without naturally having a right there." [8]

Then at the end of his life, after more than three decades

[7] For three winters (1857–1860) after his return from Europe, Melville tried his hand at public lecturing, with no great success or personal gratification. His lingering reputation as the author of *Typee* was probably a main factor in his getting sixteen engagements, the first season, through the northeast and middle west; the next year he had only ten, though they paid better; the third season, only three. This interval in his life is very thoroughly described by Merton M. Sealts, Jr., in *Melville as Lecturer* (Cambridge, Massachusetts, 1957).

[8] Letter to A. W. M. Baillie, September 10, 1864.

of silence as a teller of tales, in a groping, painful resurgence of his old narrative authority, he composed *Billy Budd.* This last of his stories has been continuously praised since its posthumous publication in 1924, its gravity and poignancy in both subject and style proving irresistible in the telling. Nevertheless I think it scarcely an exaggeration to say that *Billy Budd* remains Melville's most undervalued and persistently misinterpreted work (see below, Chapter Eight). It has been described ad infinitum as an allegory of this or that philosophical creed or religious belief, and as essentially submissive and elegiac in tone, as befits a sort of last testament. But it is not an allegory, and it is, as I read it, as confidently and positively assertive, as charged with the passion to demonstrate and explain, as anything Melville ever wrote. What it does assert, in the defining drama of its two stalwart principals, the truth-abiding captain and the "handsome sailor," is nothing less than an image of that gravely radiant virtue of spirit, that both civil and natural magnanimity, which in the last analysis is the truly exemplary feature of Melville's own character and career, and which—miraculously—survived intact to the very end.

CHAPTER ONE

MELVILLE IN HIS CAREER: 1846–1850

"... the apprehension of the absolute condition of present things as they strike the eye of the man who fears them not, though they do their worst to him. ..."—MELVILLE TO HAWTHORNE, April 1851

"FREEDOM OF VIEW"—we can see now that Hawthorne's phrase for the effectiveness of *Typee* was in a way prophetic of the whole subsequent development of Melville's powers. This freedom (of course no guarantee in itself of art or even of originality) lies at the heart of Melville's example as a writer, a source of both good and bad in his work, a cause of extraordinary inventiveness but also of extraordinary lapses of judgment and taste. It manifests itself in a variety of ways, and to list some of them is to describe no small part of Melville's distinctive practice: freedom to become wholly absorbed in what occupied his imagination, though also to lose his way in extravagances; freedom to receive impressions, to entertain and discard thoughts, to advance in understanding at his own pace and for his own materializing ends; freedom to "connect," and to discern in particular circumstances the working of larger truths and forms (a capacity, however, not only of great intelligences but also of underexposed autodidacts, who will execute astonishing leaps of insight in blissful unawareness of all that actually intervenes); freedom, as E. M. Forster remarked of Melville, from the encumbrance of a "tiresome conscience," though often, too, from the saving discipline of self-criticism; moral freedom of concentration and commitment; pragmatic freedom of language, style, performance—freedom to improvise and to borrow, and to give or not give satisfaction. These attributes are not less notable because we find them to be characteristic of a great range of American art and thought. Of the masters of our literature, perhaps only Whitman and on occasion Mark Twain strike us as having capitalized upon this native and parochial freedom of view as resourcefully as Melville. No others have realized as boldly and forcefully that "new voice" which D. H. Lawrence was to hear in the classics of American writing; no others have entered as unconstrainedly into that "original relation to the universe" which Emerson postulated for the ideal genius of the new world.

There is, we feel sure, a positive "Americanness" about the great American books. Whatever else they may do, they document in both substance and style the special character of a distinct and peculiar "civilization," with respect to which, differences of north and south, city and village, genteel and populist, refined and spontaneous, "paleface" and "redskin," are less impressive finally than the underlying family likeness. Of the equivocal forms of life this "civilization" appears to generate, Tocqueville's *Democracy in America* remains the classic analysis; it remains, also, the classic prophecy of the consequences of such patterns of existence for the human person, when the older instinct of community atrophies and the enfranchised individual is conditioned by the common impulse of a whole society to figure as a single separate *one,* a free unit. Not only does American life, Tocqueville wrote, "make every man forget his ancestors, but it hides his descendants and separates his contemporaries from him; it throws him back forever upon himself alone, and threatens in the end to confine him entirely within the solitude of his own heart."

That the significant American writers speak with the exacerbated voice of this freedom and this solitude has become a critical commonplace, whether their testimony is taken to be restrictively "American" or prophetic of the whole tendency of modern western life. Such testimony—insofar as it is that—seems to me, however, to fall into two distinct orders of importance; and the difference between them is the difference between that writing which belongs, however picturesquely, to past history, and is mainly of documentary interest to us now, and that writing which is still creatively alive to our imaginations. The one order of work lacks, in a word, an inward energy that the other has somehow come into possession of. With respect to the condition of life it speaks out from, it will seem essentially descriptive only, or submissive. It will appear to us either as having merely *endured* the determining "American" conditions, while registering, perhaps even identifying, their overwhelming presence, or as having made the endurance of them, the personal resistance to them, assimilation of them, or defeat by them, its very subject. So in Poe and in Emily Dickinson, in Hawthorne and in Henry James, we can find a half-dialectical dramatization, and in Emerson and Thoreau an exposition, usually more histrionic than reasoned, of what is really the same great subject—the fearful personal struggle for wholeness or maturity of spirit, the tense keeping or catastrophically not keeping of an intolerably lonely equilibrium. Such writers, as we happen to pay attention to them, prove to be keepers of the historically conditioned conscience we have in common with them, and we value them as such. Their testimony may indeed make up a considerable part of the sense we come to of our own historical identity. And what we may respect most in them is precisely (in Hart Crane's words) their "extraordinary capacity for surrender"—a creative surrender of course—to the fundamental sensations of the strange way of life we more than occasionally share with them, insofar as we come alive at all. But Whitman, Mark Twain, and Melville (and more recently Hart Crane himself, on a terribly reduced scale) give us something further—though they give us this much, too, in full measure. They strike us, at their best, as having done more than hold their own and keep their imaginative integrity and balance as persons, as witnesses. They strike us as having reacted to the presumptuous novelty of American experience with a corresponding imaginative freedom; as having themselves not merely registered but substantially created the stuff of life and experience that we find in their work; as having, in short, not only dramatized the common fate but mastered, even augmented it.[1]

The difference between these two orders of creative performance, though I think it is a real one, is a matter of degree only. The three nineteenth-century writers for whom I would make this further claim were, if anything, *more* dependent upon the observed particulars of common American life than the others mentioned, more "realistic," more reportorial. But it is from them that we have got the few really commodious myth-figures in our literature, and the most provocative legends for the still unfolding tapestry of our common existence—Huck Finn and his raft; the extroverted yet furtively intimate and elegiac everyman who called himself "Walt Whitman"; the whaling voyage of one Ishmael, the comic and self-destructive revenge of one Bartleby, the rage of Ahab, the sacramental embrace of Captain Vere and Billy Budd.

If I make here a further distinction and claim for Melville an

[1] The difference suggested here, though I have put it in other terms, is of course a difference of art. "A literary creation can appeal to us in all sorts of ways," Pasternak wrote in *Dr. Zhivago*, "by its theme, subject, situations, characters. But above all it appeals to us by the presence in it of art," the least particle of which "outweighs all the other ingredients in significance" and is their "heart and soul." This art, or the creating of it, is itself a product of history—and first of all of the history of the artist. And it is, in Pasternak's formulation, "something concentrated, strictly limited"—within, I assume he meant, the particulars of its own existence. But as such it is also a primary occasion *of* history; it is at least a paradigm of what history is composed of, and therefore an inexhaustible stimulus to the making of new history. It is a brave and not hollow assertion that history is still to be made.

In our own time, it scarcely needs saying, one phenomenon impressively registered by this second and lesser order of creative literature, as I have defined it, is just this struggle to achieve the further concentration and vital relevance which characterizes the first and highest order of works of art.

authority of example beyond even Twain and Whitman, this list of particular instances may begin to explain why. We do not begrudge Twain and Whitman the special perspectives, and the ultimately insulated circumstances, within which they lodge their best work—the perspective and circumstance, with Twain, of boyhood and a visionary past; with Whitman, of an idealized indolence and disengagement from consequential action. But in both cases the freedom to merge and participate is based on a freedom to withdraw intact. These two prodigies (no less) forged their creative opportunity by inventing a submissiveness to speak through which is at once natural and absolute, and which, by the condition of immunity their work marks out for itself, is strangely unexacting of the world of common undertakings and actual experience, even when most energetically in touch with it. Their great achievements are of course irreplaceable, and are not at all diminished if we point out that they do require a more than ordinary suspension of disbelief. We can hardly bear to imagine Huck Finn grown up and immersed in adult life—nor could Mark Twain;[2] no more can we imagine "Walt Whitman" attaching himself with any permanence, and to the point of common responsibility, to any of the identities he so provocatively claimed communion with—except, significantly, that of the silent wound-dresser. But Melville's legend-making, as the examples cited may suggest, is, insistently, in and of the adult historic world. I do not find that it needs the exemptions, the degree of remission from the whole conceivable aspect of the reality it fixes upon, that we gladly accord Twain's and Whitman's. And it includes their deepest responses: Melville dramatizes the judgment put upon society by the innocent suffering of those it makes its victims and outcasts not less movingly than Twain; he projects the versatility of the self, the love of comrades, and the pathos of the democracy of death as richly and compassionately as Whitman. He

[2] See Kenneth S. Lynn's interesting article, "Huck and Jim," in the *Yale Review*, XLVI (March 1958), 421–431.

also gives us, more than they, and with an unconstraint unique in American letters, the known world on its own manifold and fantastic terms. He takes us somewhat closer, within the custom of life and forms of association familiar to him, to the developed natural order of established human existence.

II

The freedom of view and personal unconstraint in Melville's work appear deeply temperamental, or constitutional. What an English admirer called, some years after his death, the "peculiar charm and bonhomie" of his writing seem to have been in good part a natural overflow of the personal vivacity and geniality emphasized in almost every account we have of him in the half-dozen years after *Typee.* On occasion these qualities could be embarrassing, in company as in his books. His Pittsfield neighbor Mrs. Sarah Morewood felt obliged to take note, writing to one of the Duyckincks (December 28, 1851), of Mr. Melville's excessive freedom in serious conversation (she intimated that it bothered her husband more than herself). She mentioned specifically his "religious views" and "irreverent language," and then a certain heedlessness or indifference, at social gatherings, to the sensibilities of others. It was just this enthusiastic indifference to propriety that had brought on the only adverse reviews of *Typee,* mostly in the religious and missionary press, and that had caused Hawthorne to go out of his way in his review to remark that the author's moral tolerance was *not* to be confused with "laxity of principle." And it was heedlessness not just according to Victorian standards. Even now, with *Omoo* (the least deliberated of Melville's books), it is possible to feel a certain thoughtlessness, or unconsidering baseness of acquiescence, in the narrator's account of drifting and mooching along the Tahiti beaches.

On those ready to respond freely, Melville's personal character made a profound impression. He met the Hawthornes in the best of circumstances—on summer holiday, in 1850, at the moment of the publication of his extraordinary essay on *Mosses from an Old Manse,* and on the confident upswing of his work on *Moby-Dick.* "Mr. Melville is a person of great ardor & simplicity," Sophia Hawthorne wrote: "a man with a true, warm heart, and a soul and an intellect, with life to his finger-tips; earnest, sincere, and reverent; very tender and *modest* . . . a very great man." She described him as "tall and erect, with an air free, brave, and manly" and "a strange, lazy glance" that "does not seem to penetrate through you, but to take you into himself." What struck her most was Melville's way of getting caught up in the occasion, the excitement and occupation of the moment: "He is all on fire with the subject that interests him" (though she noticed, too, his tact in not forcing himself upon his friends, his care "not to interrupt Mr. Hawthorne's mornings"). "When conversing, he is full of gesture and force, and loses himself in his subject. There is no grace nor polish. Once in a while, his animation gives place to a singularly quiet expression . . . an indrawn, dim look, but which at the same time makes you feel that he is at that instant taking deepest note of what is before him." But she too had to remark, as acquaintance grew, on the strangeness of his manner and address. His conversation was the more unsettling for being so inadvertently confiding: "[His] fresh, sincere, glowing mind . . . is in a state of 'fluid consciousness,' & to Mr. Hawthorne speaks his innermost about GOD, the Devil, & Life if so be he can get at the Truth for he is a boy in opinion—having settled nothing yet—informe—ingens—& it would betray him to make public his confessions & efforts to grasp,—because they would be considered perhaps impious, if one did not take in the whole scope of the case." She was speaking here of his "remarkable" letter to Hawthorne on *The House of the Seven Gables.* But her remarks apply a fortiori to Melville's published writing. How well, in fact, they fit *Moby-Dick*—its rapid changes of mood and pitch; the entire imaginative absorption at each stage of it; the poetic power of local concentration seemingly at the expense of orderly construction; the carelessly opportunistic, almost inadvertent lunges at ultimate verities; and under all these effects the temperament and voice created for Ishmael (best of Melville's many first-person narrators), who is at once a naturally effective spokesman for the author's own intuitions, and an indispensable means of letting unfold freely and commodiously the whole conceivable, still-being-conceived compass of the created action.

Of the impression Melville's personal qualities could make, and the "strangeness" in this mixture of youthfully fluid receptiveness and adult authority of response, he was himself soon enough aware; and this self-awareness surely excited him as his career advanced. It nourished his ambition and also his confidence as he found himself caught up in that process of incessant unfolding which he described to Hawthorne in the famous letter of June 29, 1851, a letter which conjecture about his "development" has scarcely got beyond. He had overreached in writing *Mardi*, but was not deeply troubled by this failure; he reacted to the poor reviews it got on both sides of the Atlantic with an easy (though untested) assurance that all this was a natural phase in the building of a great career. "Time, which is the solver of all riddles, will solve 'Mardi,'" he wrote Judge Shaw, and he assured his disenchanted London publisher that the book "will reach those for whom it is intended." He went on, however, in even more ambiguous terms, though still jauntily enough, to justify what he had done in *Mardi*, and in so doing introduced that intuition of fatality, that sense that what one did was governed by some inscrutable operation of cause and effect, which in two or three years more was to become the dominant theme of his self-accounting: "But some of us scribblers, My Dear Sir, always have a certain something unmanageable in us, that bids us do this or that, and be done it must—hit or miss."

How should he have felt otherwise? Given the rapid career as a popular author that, after the drifting interval of his sea-life, was now sweeping him along, and becoming sharply conscious of an extraordinary unfolding within himself, how could he help feeling in the grip of some strange, impersonal design? How could he keep from becoming absorbed in it and full of presentiment about it? There is indeed something mysterious—fortuitous, not to be reduced to formula—in the pattern of that career, up through the writing of *Pierre,* and (perplexment for criticism) in its curious products. What strange, original books Melville wrote, between 1846 and 1852! Even among themselves they are, each one, without precedent, however alert to this and that model our scholarship finds them. There has been much interesting speculation about the phenomenon of Melville's career *after Moby-Dick,* particularly the "alienation" from the contemporary public, and from the very vocation of literature, that so soon overtook him; but this later course his career was to follow seems much less difficult to understand (being so close to the experience of modern writers) than does its rising action. How *did* those sentences, those chapters, this book and the next one, get written? The lingering and boundless amazement which Melville describes as overtaking Israel Potter entering his long exile in the "City of Dis" seems to express his own state of mind as he looked back, after 1852, upon his own history. How easily, we feel, observing what we can of his life and temperament, he might have gone his father's or his older brother's ruined ways or the pathetic ways of his restless, voiceless children.[3] We may well imagine the years at sea to have been somehow decisive—tempering and forestalling the family instability, giving his mind something not self-engendered and self-enclosing to attach to, habituating him to a different rhythm of experience and a different measure of speech. But this brings us little closer to understanding his specific accomplishment as a writer. It is not, I repeat, as a natural phenomenon that Melville's career remains valuable to

[3] See Leyda, *The Melville Log,* and Metcalf, *Herman Melville: Cycle and Epicycle,* for family letters and history.

us, though it has its phenomenal explanations, but as a series of deliberated and achieved acts, resulting in a series of particular performances (all more or less "impromptu," as Melville said of *Typee,* at their inception) that go forward as he made them, sentence by sentence, paragraph by paragraph, chapter by chapter.

III

Melville's confidence in his vocation, unabating despite the reception of *Mardi,* was not merely wishful. He knew that the book had failed, but that his powers as a writer had leaped ahead. In the mild depression that followed the writing of *Redburn* and *White-Jacket* (and that coincided with his trip to England in the fall of 1849, the first real pause in his career since *Typee*) he no longer claimed much for *Mardi,* but accounted himself "the wiser for it," or so he told Evert Duyckinck, and he made no apologies. *Mardi* is flagrantly extemporized and synthetic in organization. Melville stuffed into it whatever in the way of information or "truth" or ingenuity of style happened to catch his eye in the "old books" he was bolting down during 1847 and 1848—Seneca, Froissart, Rabelais, Burton, Thomas Browne, Montaigne, Bougainville's *Voyage* and Frithiof's Saga, Ossian, Coleridge, David Hartley, and so on—not to mention the contents of the morning newspapers. Yet for all that, *Mardi* seemed to Hawthorne "rich" and "deep," and on the scale of a masterpiece: "It is so good that one scarcely pardons the writer for not having brooded longer over it, so as to make it a great deal better."

Long brooding was of the essence of Hawthorne's method—until, as he put it, he might overcome his own adamant and wholly realize his conception—but it was not Melville's way, except perhaps with *Billy Budd.* The richness of *Mardi* is the immediate product of the unseasoned, undistilled overflow of its author's growth of mind. Its topics and opinions, its occasions for satire and moral declaration (exuberantly taken up and hectically run through, with dialectical "yets" and "buts" crowding the short-winded argument along) are mostly thrown away in the performance. But it is nevertheless vibrant with Melville's awkwardly obtruding impulse to bear his witness and speak his truths. Stronger than any of its "ideas" is the impression it delivers of the phenomenon of the formation of ideas in the human mind, and of the situation of being acted upon by life and of having, for the sake of one's integrity of conscious being, one's intellectual manhood, to respond in measure. In *Mardi* we feel Melville's thoughts, and his very motives to thinking, taking form and gathering momentum, very little according to the requirements either of theme or of structure, but very much according to the progressive inclinings and urgings of his own immediate apprehension.

So it is in *Mardi* that the testamentary character of Melville's work begins, at considerable cost, to assert itself. This was the first of three ambitious but disorganized books, evenly spaced along the rapid cycle of his public career, in which his conception of himself (and of the writer) as a discoverer and speaker of general truths was allowed to displace rather than to complement the practical business of story-telling—a displacement that proceeds brashly and indiscriminately in *Mardi* (1847–1848), then with the tension of great personal distress and yet with impressive force and deliberation in *Pierre* (1851–1852), and then with a dry and exhaustively substantiated pessimism in *The Confidence-Man* (1856). Actually, each of these three books sets out an exceptionally "original" situation, and a plot-scheme of considerable ingenuity. Also, they are Melville's only long prose works which are not largely documentary, in substance and organization. On the other hand they suffer more than any of his other books from the positive interference of imperfectly absorbed literary models—of Rabelais in the case of *Mardi;* of *Tristram Shandy* (as Edward Rosenberry has persuasively argued) in the case of *The Confidence-Man;* and in the case of *Pierre,* of various competing precedents, from *Ham-*

let to the popular melodrama of romantic sentiment. Just those factors that gave freedom and strength to Melville's imagination —his openness to experience, his seriousness of judgment, his mimetic facility, and then his coming-of-intellectual-age so abruptly, so relatively late, and yet with so little prejudice and with a reactive mechanism of such elasticity and power—also made him especially vulnerable, just at his most ambitious, to influence of this kind, and increased his uncertainty in handling the larger forms of fiction.[4]

But it is in *Mardi,* too, that we first observe a phenomenon characteristic of all the work Melville packed into the next four years—and that is its way of gaining in achieved power from its own laboring forward. The very occupation of writing germinates, so to speak, its own most enriching motives and effects. We do well not to overlook how great a resource for all this work was Melville's progressive experience of executing it, for this was his "life" in the time of his decisive growth. So the most impressive section of *Mardi* is, I think, the last sixth of it, after its earlier undertakings—the Polynesian idylls and metaphysical debates, the religious tour of Maramma and the timely political satire on Europe and America of 1848—have been run through. The intermittently allegorical voyage across all the civil, peopled globe is now (Chapter 169, "Sailing On") admitted to have been "chartless"; and in a much-remarked passage in which the narrator pledges himself if need be to "boundless deeps" and "an utter wreck," he steers on into another world, stranger than any physical sphere—"It is the world of mind." This same shift of interest, as we shall see, is repeated on a more complex and exacting scale toward the end of *Moby-Dick,* and again between *Moby-Dick* and *Pierre.* In *Mardi* Melville was too thoroughly committed to the topical allegory, or allegories, composing the bulk of his narrative to get very far into its emergent

[4] The same excessive susceptibility to literary influence nearly brings *Moby-Dick* aground, among the pseudo-Shakespearean rhythms and rhetoric of some of Ahab's speeches.

new subject. Yet simply the thought of this "world of mind" brings a new seriousness and meditative coherence into his prose, as in philosophic Babbalanja's final discourse and renderings of the sage Bardianna—though the writing is still disagreeably rhapsodic. The most persuasive note in *Mardi* is struck in Babbalanja's description at Serenia of a living universe of spirits restlessly seeking embodiment and materializing in all men's "sad and shadowy dreams, and boundless thoughts"; as Melville apprehends it, the "world of mind" is first of all a world of actual and particular minds. In *Mardi* this image of the collective torment of all souls that have ever lived (also projected in the lyrical chapter "Dreams," and more generally in the whole drifting lagoon-and-island setting of the book) lacks the backing of a cogent story and plausible characters. But we may note that it exactly anticipates that vision of the sea as both reflecting and containing "all that we call lives and souls" upon which, in *Moby-Dick*, Melville built the beautiful and climactic chapter "The Pacific," and from which indeed, as it is also evoked in the very first chapter of *Moby-Dick*, that whole grand chronicle proceeds. And insofar, in *Mardi*, as this image incorporates an apprehension of all mankind as participating in one common existence—spiritual yet defined by physical mortality, and constrained to one fixed rhythm of aspiration and nemesis—it acts to support the hypnotic tempo of the book's closing action; it grounds the narrator's disembodied quest in at least a visionary likeness of the widest circumstance of human life and death.

IV

Within a few weeks of the publication of *Mardi* and the first disappointing reviews, Melville was again at work, and more professionally than ever. He wrote *Redburn* and *White-Jacket* in four months, between May and August of 1849, pressing ahead at the rate of at least two of his typically short and self-contained chapters a day. Once these books were in print, he professed to care very little for them—"trash" written "to buy some tobacco with," done "by the job, as a woodsawyer saws wood"; but such after-the-fact remarks protest too much, and primarily express the still further thrust of his ambition. Clearly he took pains in writing them. Each is distinguished by a purposefulness of conception and a clarity and wholeness of performance that largely make up for their slackness in general structure. There is awkwardness, but there is little tiredness or repetition. Melville did not bother to disguise the haste and improvisation of the writing: both narratives fall too often into sentences like, "I may as well glance here at . . ." or "I had almost forgotten to mention . . ." or "The allusion in the preceding chapter to the early age at which some of the midshipmen enter the Navy suggests some thoughts relative to more important considerations." But there are corresponding virtues—a new directness and appositeness of address, a degree of control over stylistic affectation, an attentively thorough and serious respect for the subject at hand—which mark altogether a distinct advance over the haphazard picturesqueness of the earlier books.

Imaginative coherence is the determining virtue of both *Redburn* and *White-Jacket*, and we may take this as the surest warrant of a consolidating talent, and of creative stamina and concentration. The data in these books, honestly and unstintingly detailed, is singular enough but not brilliantly picturesque or exotic, nor is it very systematically assembled; insofar as it holds together and comes to life, it is by the firmness of the point of view and the consistency of the coloring. Part of this new definiteness is dramatic. In both books the narrator is more solidly individualized than any Melville had yet created to speak through. The voice and the general vein of mock-solemn tenderfoot comedy devised for the boy Redburn are every bit as accomplished as, to take an exactly contemporary parallel, what Dickens devised for David Copperfield, and very much more satisfactory than the insufferable accents imposed, four years later, on Esther Summerson in *Bleak House*.[5] And in the narrator of *White-Jacket*, buoyantly good-natured, self-respecting, compassionate, speculatively fanciful, the pattern is set for *Moby-Dick*'s Ishmael, though only sketchily realized.

But these achievements are a little mechanical, or self-enclosed. They stand somewhat apart from the full charge of argument and emotion that each book eventually generates. As the narratives progress, the self-characterizing voices of Wellingborough Redburn and the main-topman White Jacket tend to dissolve into an explanatory and interpretive voice which must be taken as the author's own. The fault, however, is technical and not imaginative, if that distinction may be made. Though both books thus speak with a somewhat divided voice, one part dramatic and suitable to the projected narrator, the other discursive and entrusted with the author's further purposes, each voice is persuasive in its own right, and, more important, there is no real inconsistency between them: they speak from a uniform apprehension of things. The difference is not one of attitude or judgment but of position; the one voice is used for direct participation in events, the other for recollecting them from a distance and reflecting on their significance.

The leading action of *Redburn* is the young hero's progress into "the cold charities" of the adult world, as encountered aboard the merchant ship *Highlander* and in New York, Liverpool, and London—"a moving world," it is called, that provides neither security nor equilibrium except for those privileged to buy them or strong enough to contrive their own. In a rough way the book registers Melville's sense of his own growth and experience. But it is only casually autobiographical. And it does not, I think, make its impression as a novel of "initiation," as has been claimed; its hero's experience is simply not given to us in sufficient depth. In the course of the events related, he

[5] Serial publication of *David Copperfield* began in London in early May of 1849, just as Melville, in New York, was beginning to write *Redburn*. The coincidence is remarkable, though consideration of sailing schedules pretty well eliminates the possibility of influence.

appears to have grown wiser and stronger, or at least more resilient and less vulnerable, but there is no spiritual transformation; certainly he does not "fall," and is not "reborn." Rather, such progress in awareness as he seems to make is natural and cumulative, however painful; it is a function of the particular course of circumstances and transactions which his narrative describes. This point deserves some emphasis, with respect to Melville's subsequent career. Fourth in order of composition among his books, *Redburn* is the first to give free expression to that circumstantial sense of human character which was soon to become habitual and preoccupying with him—the sense that the moral pattern within which any man's character mysteriously enacts its life is essentially contingent rather than connate or self-made, and that its aspect and direction are determined simply by the successive accidents of this or that life-history. So the narrative gives us not only a more fully characterized hero than we have yet had from Melville but correspondingly a more objective and matter-of-fact rendering of the given, familiar world he makes his way through and of the kinds of behavior that may in general be expected of its inhabitants.

With *Redburn's* deepening intimations of the moral character of humankind—intimations which, though not integrally joined to the story of the young hero's "first voyage," are wholly consistent with it—Melville's work moves strongly out of its apprenticeship toward the bold authority of its mature example. The notation of a certain "recklessness and sensualism of character" among the common sailors, the beggary and murderous destitution of Liverpool, the panic and inhumanity of fine gentlemen confronted by steerage pestilence on the return voyage, the petty cheating of the Captain, the domination of the spiteful, blasphemous Jackson ("a Cain afloat") over the rest of the crew—all the observation in *Redburn* of this world and its life obviously hangs together, and stands in fact at the edge of a consistent symbolism. The narrative does not shy off from its deeper feelings and wider implications. Human beings are forthrightly identified as they are found and as they may therefore be imagined; they are "starvelings" and "misanthropes," walled up in neighborhoods where "common iniquities are virtues too lofty for the infected gorgons and hydras to practice" and where God's word goes forever unspoken, but they are nevertheless, to compassionate attention, "His children" all. "Adam and Eve!" the narrator declares, "may it be no part of your immortality to look down upon the world ye have left," for the sight of it "would be a parental torment indeed." For "surrounded as we are by the wants and woes of our fellowmen, and yet given to follow our own pleasures, regardless of their pains, are we not like people sitting up with a corpse, and making merry in the house of the dead?" As the burden of statement which the narrative rises to assume becomes too weighty for the boy Redburn's voice, it is taken up by passages like these, of rhetorical elaboration and climax, in which all readers of Melville will recognize his distinctive style. The passages just quoted occur, in fact, in successive chapter endings (Chapters 35–39), in each of which factual narrative is lifted into peroration; it is in *Redburn* and *White-Jacket* that the rounded Melvillean chapter fixes itself as his most natural and adaptable unit of composition.

White-Jacket is the harder of these two books to place critically. It is looser and more wayward in form, but it is also larger in compass and more resonant in its promise. Melville himself thought better of it than of *Redburn*, and never spoke of it quite so dismissingly (in part because he was hopeful that its critique of man-of-war discipline might contribute to the humanization of the American naval service). But it is commonly felt to be the less accomplished work of the two [6]—more diffuse and slack-paced, more negligent in directing and holding attention, leaning too heavily on piecemeal charm of manner and, worse, on a merely piecemeal symbolism (as of the jacket, or of

[6] See, for instance, Newton Arvin, *Herman Melville* (New York, 1950), 110ff.

the man-of-war as a microcosm), and marred as a piece of narrative writing by journalistic sermonizing which, though effective in itself, is not formally assimilated. We may notice, however, that these same faults may be attributed to *Moby-Dick*, for which indeed *White-Jacket* now appears to us as something of a trial run. With respect to Melville's powers of sustained composition, it marks an important step forward. It gives freer play than *Redburn* to that confident mastery of the things and facts of human occupation, and of their proper names, which Melville would soon call upon to buoy up the long elaborations of the *Pequod's* whaling voyage. And where most of *Redburn* is held down to a narrow, stifling sense of human nature sordidly closed in on itself, *White-Jacket* is deliberately and to a degree contrapuntally flung out along the kind of spacious, oceanic, round-the-world course which, in *Moby-Dick*, serves to provide a setting authenticatingly vast and prodigious for the melodrama of Captain Ahab. The boldness of the design suggests how Melville's ambition as a writer of books was for the time keeping pace with his ambition as a declarer of truths.

I suspect that the difficulty criticism has had with *White-Jacket* is principally one of finding a standard to judge it by. Contemporary preoccupation with the art of the novel and its special norms may be at fault in this. For *White-Jacket* is not a novel, despite an opening chapter which, as spiritedly as the opening chapter of *Moby-Dick*, announces a character and promises a story, and despite the narrator's intermittent projection of himself as an Ishmael or a Jonah. Its motives are chiefly documentary and polemical; it systematically displays the operation of a man-of-war and attacks abuses in the treatment of the crew. And yet it is a work of imagination, as Dana's *Two Years* and Cooper's *Ned Myers* are not. What other narrative of an actual voyage is as effusively and gaily inventive? Also, the impression it renders is "complete," as V. S. Pritchett has commented, and it grows tiresome only as the effort at completeness of statement may prove tiresome in any discourse; this is a measure of its superiority as a finished book not only to *Redburn,* where the narrative line is tidier, but also to *Israel Potter* and *The Confidence-Man,* where the exposition is at times more brilliant or more profound but insufficiently persistent. More surely than any of Melville's earlier books, *White-Jacket* grows to its strength, generating its own resources over a longer, steadier haul. The three chapters against flogging (Chapters 34–36), following a vivid scene of punishment at the mast and rising to an impressive eloquence, show a new power and suppleness of argument—argument that is at once reasoned, analogizing, circumstantial, and fervent—as well as an increasing sureness with prose cadence. The last chapter, too, is worth noting. Though something of an afterthought in the scheme of the narrative, it easily carries through the kind of emphatic imaginative conceit (of the world as a frigate sailing under sealed orders) to which Melville's versatile intelligence was now reaching out for its boldest undertakings.

None of Melville's books was better received than *White-Jacket.* The slightly patronizing attitude which even the more generous notices of his first work betray gave way now to plain and solid respect. One after another of the reviews, particularly in England, treated him as a figure to be reckoned with in contemporary literature. The appraisal in *John Bull* is not unrepresentative: "an improving and vastly improved writer . . . who, without any abatement of his rich and ever sparkling wit, has obtained the mastery of his own fancy." Much of the comment on *White-Jacket* would be perfectly appropriate to *Moby-Dick:* ". . . wondrous forms and images float before us; the wild waste of waters is stirred with a spiritual life; while real men and actions, in constant movement on shipboard, loom out palpably through the gorgeous mist. . . . You must look at the whole from a distance, and take in the entire design in its full grandeur and color of composition, if you would appreciate its true character." [7] The familiar Melvillean manner—the "super-abundant fancy" and "free-and-easy" style, as it was

[7] This notice, it must be said, appeared in *Bentley's Miscellany,* the house organ of the book's London publisher.

described in the reviews—was gaining general acceptance. A few reviewers were still bothered by it; the same notice in *John Bull* found in *White-Jacket* "far too great a freedom in touching upon sacred subjects." On the other hand even the strait-laced *Biblical Repository and Classical Review,* after enumerating "the author's characteristic faults—a swaggering air, extravagant speech, and outrageous sentiment, profane expressions . . . and a reckless care-for-nothing manner of life"—had to grant the book a "wonderful," a "heart-rending" power.

What we can see now, if we do try to "take in the entire design," is the extent to which this accomplished power is a product of the book's honest argument with itself, an argument conducted feelingly on both sides and if not resolved then not evaded either. Two formally unfused conceptions direct the narrative. Seen in the large, in a "free, broad, off-hand, bird's eye, and, more than all, impartial" view, the organized life of the great man-of-war is shown as splendid and heroic, and all the ship's company are "noble fellows and hearts of oak"; but in immediate detail this life is also shown as cruel, debased, demoralizing, even "unmanning." (I think one can plot through *White-Jacket* a sporadic effort to bring the two conceptions together.) Eventually a gathering sense of the kind of picture his materials really compose subverts the narrator's initially romantic design for it. "I let nothing slip, however small," he will say, but certain grim facts reduce him to evasiveness and indirection. Yet, "I would not be like the man, who, seeing an outcast perishing by the roadside, turned about to his friend, saying, 'Let us cross the way; my soul so sickens at this sight that I cannot endure it.'" The office of stem-to-stern exposition he has imposed on himself may become repugnant to him, but he will abide it to the end.

In the process of writing Melville found himself going imaginatively deeper into the matter of navy discipline than does his own not always unpeevish polemic against it. What he attacked in one voice, he came near to accepting in another. He had to allow that in the nature of its uses a warship would "ever remain a picture of much that is tyrannical and repelling in human nature." "Sooner might you tame the grizzly bear of Missouri than humanise a thing so essentially cruel and heartless." The pressure of this double awareness does not, however, tempt Melville into casuistries of reconciliation; he remains true to his observation and his findings. He does not argue that injustice is necessary or unavoidable; in no way is "the general ignorance or depravity of any race of men to be alleged as an apology for tyranny over them"; but the truth remains—and it is with this truth that *White-Jacket* closes—that "the worst of our evils we blindly inflict upon ourselves; our officers cannot remove them even if they would." Nothing more surely marks Melville's emergence in this book as a writer potentially of the first rank than, first, his power to hold apparently contradictory discoveries in mind at once, in free solution, and then his readiness to ransack everything he knew to explain them and to articulate them, without prejudice, as part of one vital and reasonable scheme of existence—both the sordidness of most men and the unassailable manhood of certain individuals, both the splendors of a man-of-war's ocean progress and the "sinister vein of bitterness" that runs through it all. His summing-up, when it comes, has the telling weight of truly impartial and objective demonstration: "But we have seen that a man-of-war is but this old-fashioned world of ours afloat, full of all manner of characters—full of strange contradictions; and though boasting some fine fellows here and there, yet, upon the whole, charged to the combings of her hatchways with the spirit of Belial and all unrighteousness."

CHAPTER TWO

MELVILLE IN HIS CAREER:

1850–1856

". . . a mind which by becoming really profound in itself, grew skeptical of all tendered profundities. . . ."—*Pierre,* XXVI, ii

THE SENSE of life-in-general registered in *White-Jacket* strikes us as whole and assured. Nothing, certainly, in Melville's subsequent writings will gainsay it. The equanimity with which he can address this world's "strange contradictions," and assert toward the end of his book that "what we call Fate is even, heartless, and impartial" and that "ourselves are fate," or that "there are no mysteries outside of ourselves," is neither complacent nor despairing, and would not be out of keeping in the grand scheme of *Moby-Dick.* His satisfaction in discovering how the "something unmanageable" in his own nature appears to be general among mankind does not seem spiteful; nor does he take personal credit for having found this out and freely proclaimed it. Indeed his letters of 1849 were already sounding a different, deeper note. It is as though he was now aware that he had not yet come into his own full experience of these moral truths; that he was only on the threshold of those ultimate personal developments which it is a main part of the virtue of moral philosophies to comprehend; that he had just begun to learn the full cost of his own exhilarating freedom of view.

His obsession with personal frankness, and, correspondingly, with the necessity of silence, begins to take hold at about this time. The conviction rose in him that behind the deepest utterance of the sincerest of writers there were unspoken secrets of understanding, in which the real mysteries of existence remained locked up. "Even Shakespeare," he wrote Evert Duyckinck, in March of 1849, "was not a frank man to the uttermost. And, indeed, who in this intolerant universe is, or can be?" A few months later, peddling *White-Jacket* among London publishing offices, he expressed himself more violently: "What a madness & anguish it is, that an author can never—under no conceivable circumstances—be at all frank with his readers." "Madness" may not be only hyperbole; one learns to take Melville at his word. Hearing of the insanity of Charles Fenno Hoffman, he wrote Duyckinck that "in all of us lodges the same fuel to light the same fire." A man of letters like Hoffman was "just the man to go mad—imaginative, voluptuously inclined, poor, unemployed, in the race of life distanced by his inferiors . . . without a port or haven in the universe to make." The self-premonition seems unmistakable. Two years later, in the throes of writing *Moby-Dick*, the note sounded here was to become more poignantly confessional: "My dear Sir," he announced to Hawthorne, "a presentiment is on me,—I shall at last be worn out and perish, like an old nutmeg-grater." And in the same letter we find the famous précis of his whole inward history: "Until I was twenty-five, I had no development at all. From my twenty-fifth year I date my life. Three weeks have scarcely passed, at any time between then and now, that I have not unfolded within myself. But I feel that I am now come to the inmost leaf of the bulb, and that shortly the flower must fall to the mould." The fear that all his books were "botches," and the new anxieties that underlay his letters to his publishers, were not due solely to his perception of the "intolerance" of ordinary men (to whom "Truth is ridiculous"), nor even to this new intuition that his own imaginative life was coming full term. They sprang from a further sense of the final untrustworthiness of the profoundest testimony, including his own. It might be, he suggested to Hawthorne, that God Himself "cannot explain his own secrets." It might be that "perhaps, after all, there is *no* secret." Yet all that makes us think that there is remains, and must be spoken. He would follow Hawthorne, he wrote, and stand with him, as one in the "chain of God's posts round the world," in the attempt to render "the tragicalness of human thought in its own unbiassed, native, and profounder workings" —so he praised Hawthorne for having done in *The House of the Seven Gables*—but he would do so with less and less assurance that these workings could ever be encompassed and explained.

It is altogether characteristic of Melville's development that these dark presentiments are for a time set out in increasingly pungent, vigorous, and explicit prose. In *Redburn* the mercurial behavior of Harry Bolton leads the narrator to declare, "We are all curious creatures, as everyone knows." Another year and a half of exposure to his own intensifying humors gave a new bite to this notion: "We are all queer customers, Mr. Duyckinck, you, I, & everybody else in the world." A great part of Melville's virtue as a writer (but also of the "considerable tiresomeness" D. H. Lawrence complained of) is that he does not let go of an idea until he has completed his affirmation of the whole experienced truth of it; in the process contradictions, incongruities, violations of decorum must fall as they will. So in *Moby-Dick*, which occupied him for most of the next two years (1850–1851), two strong motives out of his own accelerating growth go forward side by side—an objective and circumstantial apprehension of the nature of "this world," such as had been lined out in earnest in *Redburn* and *White-Jacket*; and a newer, more inward premonition of some "fall of valor in the soul," some besetting natural fatality athwart the career of "every man who feels his soul in him, which but few men do." As in the life-cycle of one of Toynbee's great civilizations, an imperial aggrandizement and some as yet unspecified disaster show their features, in the thrust of his imagination, side by side.

II

So much has been written about *Moby-Dick,* and demonstrated on this side and that in such abundant detail, that the few things to be said here may be said fairly briefly. My concern with the book in this chapter is not to anatomize it but simply to place it in the sequence of its author's career. Melville's masterpiece is a work of enormous and self-engendering ambitiousness; a work also, in content and in form, of improvisation. These two facts are fundamental in its organization. It was undertaken from a still fresh and still strengthening confidence in the feeling of intellectual mastery over the observed ways of "this world," but it was finished under severe nervous strain and in a state of self-conscious uncertainty, violently compensated for in the writing. This uncertainty colors all the late stages of the story, where the focus is most insistently upon Ahab. It may be felt in the overwrought style, especially in the theatrical mannerisms adopted to dramatize Ahab's willful madness. It even unsteadies to a degree the drive and pace of the magnificently staged climax—"the finest piece of dramatic writing in American literature," according to F. O. Matthiessen—as the gestures and declarations devised for Ahab continue to pile up. And it presages, we know, the miscarriage of *Pierre.* We observe, too, that this long closing section of *Moby-Dick,* the most troublesome in content and (except for the chase itself) the least surely executed, is also the most labored and strained in its recourse to literary models, notably the treacherous models of romantic allegory and Shakespearean melodrama. Granting that Ahab's story has moments of utmost poignancy, and that his part in the action is pivotal, we may still say that the greatness of the book is secured by other means technically than those used to render the mad Captain's figure and mind. It is rather secured, first, by the narrative in his own voice of the "whaling voyage by one Ishmael," Melville's boldest and heartiest undertaking in the mode of the first-person adventure chronicle, and, secondly, by the encyclopedic exposition of all the business and circumstance of sperm-whaling, an exposition which is consciously "universal" in its effort at completeness, its open-minded and exploratory pursuit of analogies, and its cumulative appeal to an ideal conception of the whole sensible nature of life in "this world."

Above all, *Moby-Dick*, both as a work of narrative art and as a document in testimony, has the ring of an immense authority. We feel that what is being said has taken into account the whole imaginable scope of the matter, has dodged nothing and asked no concessions, and is based on an apprehension of things that will not be easily astonished. This of course is the large effect that the manner assigned to Ishmael is meant to have on us. The physical vastness and strangeness of the setting, and the actions necessitated by it or resulting from it, are constantly before us, and are evoked in a suitably heraldic and yet familiar and easy way—sometimes whimsically, as in an aside on the irregularity of mail "between here and New Guinea"; sometimes fancifully, as with the ocean-spanning musk of the Salem girls; sometimes in calculated splendor, as in the *Pequod's* progress into the China Seas and the Pacific; sometimes in all of these ways at once, as in the spectacular chapter in praise of Nantucket; but always, as each of these examples suggests, through specific names and facts. These are among the passages everyone recalls, and simply to list them and others like them is a fair way to make one's claim for the sweep and grandeur of the book. It may be less of a commonplace to point out that the sense of historical dimension is summoned up not much less strongly. Consider, for example, the documentary extracts, from all times and in thirteen languages, that serve as prologue; or the analogies repeatedly drawn to great national actions like the maraudings of Alexander or Hannibal, the flooding of the Netherlands, the Mexican War and the Erie Canal; or, most appropriately, the recurrent invocation of famous ocean-voyagers and exploration-chroniclers of past times, and of the whole long era of European expansion across the world. In both dimensions, the physical or geographical and the historical, what is centrally kept in view is the fantastic energy and variety of common human enterprise. So set off, the heroic actions and lurid imaginings that the book abounds in seem perfectly in keeping without ceasing to be marvelous. The madness of an Ahab is merely a matter of circumstance and degree. The more the narrative shows of the multitudinous wonders of earthly existence, the more effectively it delivers its assertions of the essential nature of "this world" and of what "some men" (that phrase, too, recurs like an epic formula) have been capable of, and the more authoritative are its appeals to the stuff of mythology, religion, and primary philosophy.[1]

Uniquely in our literature *Moby-Dick* makes its strong, sure, humorous, masculine poetry out of customary human occupations and enterprise, out of the settled craft of carpenters and blacksmiths and the commercial adventuring of speculative capitalism as well as the more fabulous or prodigious exploits of hunters and harpooneers, and all of these side by side with the formulations of prophets and sages and the familiar experience of common souls. Uniquely, too, as Lawrence thought, the book is suffused with a sense of the vastness and mystery of nonhuman life—"the sheer naked slidings of the elements." Melville was not the first writer nor the last to give voice to the protestant-romantic lust for the naked, fundamental, and perhaps nameless truth at the heart of being. This treacherous motive did not cut him off, however, from the details of experience, from fact and from natural feeling. Nor did it ever quite betray him into the kind of programmatic abstractness that coarsens the witness-bearing even of a Blake or a Lawrence. His

[1] The surer also its rhetoric. Diction and syntax, in the full, long, descriptive-meditative sentences, are admirably managed, but the rapid pace from one to the next is not less decisive. Phrase by phrase, the writing in *Moby-Dick* responds as never before in Melville's work, and perhaps never, quite, again, to the story's and the testimony's jointly accumulating pressure.

concern for the peculiar nature of "some deep men" leads him, in *Moby-Dick,* to speak in terms of a general "life of the soul"; but it should also be observed that what the narrative mostly sets before us are the particular lives of particular souls in the context of particular life-histories. What these men are is all that has happened to them in the actual world, the reality of which it is Melville's distinctive genius never to let us doubt. Conversely, what is ascribed to fate, or to God, or to the nature of things, is never more than what his characters' demonstrated experience of this reality might naturally have brought into mind. Life is displayed in *Moby-Dick* as harsh, violent, laborious, chancy, long, inequitable, fate-ridden, overwhelming; it appears profoundly disrespectful of persons and indifferent to private fortune or sorrow; it is tragic, and it is disinheriting. At the same time, in the very energy and detail of the narrative, and in the behavior of its personae, we are given a more-than-countervailing representation of human resourcefulness. Against these precisely measured odds we are the more impressed by what is shown us of the freedom and efficacy of the courageous and strong—the readiness of an Ishmael to try all things and achieve what he can, or of an Ahab to go titanically mad and elect his own spectacular fate.[2]

But with respect to just this large apprehension of the life of "this world" and the doings of "some men" in it, there are, as the narrative moves to its climax, significant shifts of emphasis, which roughly parallel the changes and the new starts in the tactics of presentation, and which are indicative, one feels, of the personal crisis that the hard work of finishing the book was bringing to a head. Not the least remarkable aspect of *Moby-Dick* is that it does survive these forced shifts of emphasis and treatment. It survives, that is, Melville's aggrandizing impulse to use his narrative as a kind of incantatory wisdom-journal. In

[2] It is no accident that the figure of Bulkington, perfectly rendered in one famous "six-inch chapter" as the very "demigod" of this restless freedom, has loomed so large in comment on *Moby-Dick*.

these later chapters the phrase "this world" is increasingly overlaid with tendentious modifiers—"this wilful world," "this slippery world," "the step-mother world," "a wicked, miserable world," and so on—most of them, it is true, projected out of Ahab's rising passion. Similarly the heraldic place given to a Bulkington early in the book is occupied toward the end by figures like the carpenter and blacksmith, the free self-possessed hero giving way to these broken remnants of humanity with "death-longing eyes" and nothing more than some "unaccountable, cunning life-principle" left within them. The way of presenting Ahab also changes—and is in fact one cause of these other changes. In the last hundred pages he is much more constantly at the active center of things than earlier in the narrative, and we are given a considerably more intimate and inward view of him. Yet he never ceases, even here, to be essentially static and unchangeable in character, a figure sometimes for awe and sometimes for pity but never quite for full tragic sympathy. The focus of Melville's intensifying concern to define absolutely the life-process of the human soul now falls almost uninterruptedly upon Ahab, but the effect of this concentration is curiously abstractive. The ideas that gather around him compete almost too strenuously, for our attention, with the figure embodying them (here again we observe telltale shifts of phrasing, as from "some men" to "man" or to the conception of "high abstracted man alone"). To a critical degree coherent characterization, within the appointed frame of the drama, is subordinated to the author's own pursuit of universal truths.

So it is in just these late stages that *Moby-Dick* moves most deliberately toward the mode of allegory. This mutation was not on the whole a happy one for the best exercise of Melville's narrative talent. It appears, however, to have pleased the Hawthornes. Melville was lucky in having two such first readers for *Moby-Dick* as Nathaniel and Sophia Hawthorne; their appreciation was indeed, as he wrote them, a "glorious gratutity." But insofar as they "intimated the part-and-parcel allegoricalness of the whole" to him, and mentioned approvingly the various "particular subordinate allegories," they in effect gave their blessing to what was shakiest in the book's ad hoc structure, and thus to the direction in which its author's ambitions were now carrying him. The terms of their approval must be acknowledged as having contributed at least indirectly to the overweening misadventure of *Pierre*—upon which Melville now embarked almost without catching breath.

III

About this misadventure, which was decisive in the progress of his career, there is a certain air of inevitability. We have a few revealing glimpses into Melville's state of mind at this time, at the end of his intense and engrossing labor on *Moby-Dick*—as he talks through the night with Hawthorne of "all possible and impossible matters," or writes Hawthorne the strained, soaring, not wholly coherent letter of mid-November 1851, with its unanswerable questions and its inadmissible assumptions of some extraordinary intimacy or "infinite fraternity of feeling." [3] To Mrs. Morewood in Pittsfield, his condition was very simply a "morbid excitement which will soon injure his health." Her letter to George Duyckinck of December 28, 1851, gives us a symptomatic picture of Melville during the writing of *Pierre:* "now so engaged in a new work as frequently not to leave his room till dark in the evening when he for the first time during the whole day partakes of solid food. . . ."

At this climax of his explosive inward growth, two apprehensions took command of his thought—first, that he now fully understood the order of the world's existence, and had therefore some power of imaginative ascendancy over it; but, also, that

[3] "Whence come you, Hawthorne? By what right do you drink from my flagon of life? And when I put it to my lips—lo, they are yours and not mine."

he now fully understood the accidental, contingent nature of his own particular being, his profoundest mind and soul, and therefore had no real independence of action at all. The first apprehension made him bold to strike harder and probe deeper than ever yet at the very "axis of reality," in the way that seemed to him to define the special genius of Shakespeare. The second taught him that he had no real position to strike from, or at least none from which he could gain the one kind of hearing that now seemed worthwhile—among that "aristocracy of the brain" to which he confessed to Hawthorne his own sense of a calling, or in "that small but high hushed world" which he had made Ishmael declare himself "not unreasonably ambitious of." His will to create and control was eroded by self-doubts; his confidence in his powers as a writer was beset by all the "thousand inconceivable finicalnesses of small pros and cons about imaginary fitnesses, and proprieties, and self-consistencies" that much of *Pierre,* in just this overwrought idiom, is exhaustively devoted to.

Yet not even in *Pierre* did the rush of Melville's presumption, or the anguish of doubt, overset his imagination's fundamental honesty and objectivity. He held as doggedly to "truth" in piecing out this most confessional of his books as he had in documenting the naval service or the whaling industry. "With no son of man," he truthfully enough told Hawthorne, "do I stand upon any etiquette or ceremony"—and least of all with himself. The determining subject of *Pierre* corresponds to his own most pressing personal history, for it is "that maturer and larger interior development" within his hero which is predicated in so many words at the outset of the main narrative.[4] In composing *Pierre* Melville laid his hand to various means of emphasis and elaboration—analogies with the history of Christ, allusions to the *Inferno* and *Hamlet,* intimations from transcendentalist philosophy and the myths of Memnon and En-

[4] This phrase occurs in the first of a series of carefully worded sentences of foreshadowing explanation, in section ii, Book I.

celadus, not to mention a dreary assortment of stock Romantic emblems (mirrors and portraits, a mystic guitar, fair and dark female angels, and so on)—and all of this has resulted in as many philosophical, allegorical, and psycho-biographical interpretations as may be imagined. But his main theme is Pierre's development in natural consciousness and insight, and the good writing in the book is never far off it. For literary history, then, the significant fact is simply that at this extremity of personal crisis Melville plunged, in his first essay outside the form of first-person narrative, into the prime Romantic subject of the "growth of the mind." And though his inward agitation and his inordinate personal stake in the undertaking wrecked the book formally, they also were what gave it its almost saving virtues—the "force and subtlety of thinking and unity of purpose" praised by the *Graham's* reviewer, and intermittently a passionate exactness of psychological notation which can bear comparison with its great Romantic prototype, *The Prelude.*

From a secure base in first-person narrative Melville had improvised for most of *Moby-Dick* a spectacularly effective formal solution. But the apparatus of Romantic melodrama that he now turned to proved unreconcilable with his deeper purposes in what he chose to call "this book of sacred truth." The odd divisions and sub-divisions of the novel speak for Melville's difficulties. There are twenty-six "Books," so-called, of which several run to fewer than ten pages, while others are broken into half a dozen or more sub-sections; also, there is an immoderate use of short-winded, discontinuous paragraphing, as if the narrative was repeatedly gathering itself for some radical new departure. If anything good can be said of this structure, it might be of the abrupt transitions it makes possible into exploratory metaphor and analogy, such as in long stretches of *Pierre* wholly supersede narrative incident. By these interpolations Melville seeks, as it were, to canvass the surrounding possibilities, and to generalize the meager and usually implausible events of the story and assert their participation in some broadly significant order of things. I am not thinking here of set-piece digressions like the Enceladus passage or Plinlimmon's pamphlet on "chronometricals and horologicals." I have in mind rather the fitful, tangent-following succession of short metaphoric paragraphs, or of overloaded single sentences and clauses, in which themes and ideas never quite satisfactorily embodied in the fantastic action of the novel come boiling up from below.[5] But this kind of structure, and the style that carries it forward, would at best be suitable only to some other genre, such as the long Wordsworthian narrative-reflective poem, in which the job would be to represent a uniform series of moral and psychological incidents with sensuous force and precision, rather than to round out a coherent story. The organization of *Pierre* is really not dramatic at all, but at once lyrical and expository. The book proceeds by strophe and antistrophe—Melville was in fact to grow so impatient of his plot that at one late juncture a new sequence of "most momentous events" is simply dropped

[5] A passage in Book xxv, section ii, is typical of the way in which most of *Pierre* gets itself told. Here Pierre's cousin Glen and his prospective brother-in-law Frederic have come into the field against him: "What then would those two boiling bloods do? Perhaps they would patrol the streets; and at the first glimpse of lonely Lucy, kidnap her home. Or if Pierre were with her, then smite him down by hook or crook, fair play or foul; and then, away with Lucy! Or if Lucy systematically kept her room, then fall on Pierre in the most public way, fell him, and cover him from all decent recognition beneath heaps and heaps of hate and insult; so that broken on the wheel of such dishonor, Pierre might feel himself unstrung, and basely yield the prize.

"Not the gibbering of ghosts in any old haunted house; no sulphurous and portentous sign at night beheld in heaven, will so make the hair to stand, as when a proud and honorable man is revolving in his soul the possibilities of some gross public and corporeal disgrace. It is not fear; it is pride-horror, which is more terrible than any fear. Then, by tremendous imagery, the murderer's mark of Cain is felt burning on the brow, and the already acquitted knife blood-rusts in the clutch of the anticipating hand.

"Certain that these two youths must be plotting something furious against him; with the echoes of their scorning curses . . ."—and so on through half a dozen more intricately specifying subordinate clauses, after which the main statement—"Pierre could not but look forward to wild work very soon to come"—is fairly ludicrous.

onto the page in outline form (XXI, ii). Even the grotesquely inventive vocabulary of *Pierre,* with its participial nouns and adverbs and its bizarre coinages ("slidings," "slopings," "over-layingly," "perennialness," "universalness," "smilingness," "transmittedness," "vacant whirlingness of the bewilderingness," and the like), is a poet's vocabulary, aimed at some ideal denomination of its subjects according to their determinative mode of being. The effect of this vocabulary is mostly disastrous. But it is fair to note that magnificent precedent for at least one of its idiosyncrasies may be found, again, in Wordsworth:

> . . . those obstinate questionings
> Of sense and outward things,
> Fallings from us, vanishings,
> Blank misgivings. . . .

With a work as freakish as *Pierre,* comparisons may be helpful. It is instructive to put beside it another novel of the period, Meredith's *Ordeal of Richard Feverel* (1859), in which, too, the organization is essentially discursive and lyrical rather than narrative or dramatic. Like Melville the young Meredith was undertaking to be something more than a story-teller; and he used the gross scheme of romantic melodrama as an instrument of truth-telling and moral indoctrination. When near the beginning of *Pierre* we find Melville opposing "the demon Principle" to an idyll of youthful summer love, the resemblance appears very close indeed. Both novels have much to say about the equivocality of worldly affairs and the distress that results for fine spirits—Meredith's, it must be granted, with a steadier humor. But this resemblance is mostly between what is weakest or most commonplace in the two books, both of which lean too readily, when imagination is slack, on a kind of poeticized wisdom-mongering. "All round and round does the world lie as in a sharp-shooter's ambush, to pick off the beautiful illusions of youth, by the pitiless cracking rifles of the realities of the age": it perhaps will take a discriminating ear to say with confidence which one this sentence is taken from. But in a round view, differences in temper and direction are immediately apparent. The confessional and meditative intensity of Melville's narrative is quite absent from Meredith's, which condescends to its materials, and is altogether less curious about them. Where *Richard Feverel* stays fastened to a set of a priori moral precepts which the particulars of the novel are merely allowed to illustrate, *Pierre* is exploratory and introspective, at whatever cost. In Meredith's handling, romantic love, or the first love of the young and healthy, is an absolute virtue. The agency by which other healthy virtues are released, it is itself whole and uncontingent. But for Melville the action of love belongs to the natural history of the developing soul, and must participate in the ambiguity of that history, though standing for a time at its vital center. And insofar as love is thus the force by which the human person grows into his main life and emerges, if ever he does, out of "empty nominalness" into the "vital realness" of unsheltered experience, it must be for him a deepest pain and torment.

At the center of Melville's conception of his hero's life-history is this natural sequence of inward growth. The insistence on explaining in minute detail every inflection of motive in Pierre's mind, and every new position and rhythmic phase in the mechanics of his responsiveness, follows from this conception—though when the method resulting is applied to a character's most casual or merely prudential decisions, it becomes grotesque. At its most effective, however, it gives us with considerable cogency something like an affective, not to say dramatic, theory of knowledge; it provides, that is, a working display of the process by which thoughts are formed and the commitments of feeling actually entered into within the human mind. At this level of demonstration *Pierre* is an extraordinary performance.[6] Its delivered strength is not in its ideas-as-such but in this central rehearsal of the organic life of the soul, or what others in Melville's day were calling the natural history of intellect. Even the sensational plot serves chiefly for demonstrative emphasis; so the situation of incest, curiously underplayed, is principally a sign of the fearful tautologies of consciousness as it goes its natural course, and especially of its bottomless capacity for self-violence. The universal distrust that breaks on Pierre; the sense of "the ambiguities" of existence (or of "the tragic convertibility between truth and falsehood, good and evil" which Charles Feidelson, I think misleadingly, has called the backbone of the novel); the vivid projections of nervous disorder and of the insanity produced by the encroachments of ungoverned memory—all come as the consequence of a natural and irreversible growth of mind, in the "boundless" expansion of its single life. And if we say that in themselves the assertions of philosophical opinion in *Pierre* are not deeply impressive, holding our attention only as they happen to speak for this main action, we are simply being consistent with the book's strongest "philosophical" intuition: "For there is no faith, and no stoicism, and no philosophy, that a mortal man can possibly evoke, which will stand the final test of a real impassioned onset of Life and Passion upon him. . . . For Faith and philosophy are air, but events are brass. Amidst his gray philosophizings, Life breaks upon a man like the morning."

IV

The clarity and firmness of this declaration are not communicated, unfortunately, to the whole narrative scheme. Beyond this point, three-quarters of the way along, *Pierre* runs downhill. Its great theme is again muffled by the preposterousness of

[6] Particularly striking in this respect are two long sequences painstakingly analyzing the impact upon Pierre's mind of a single new transforming apprehension, in both instances of the knowledge of dark Isabel and what she portends for him (IV, i to V, ii, and IX–X).

the story, which is finished out by main force, in haste and self-doubt. And from this time forward, what we know of Melville's whole career makes a corresponding impression on us, despite the brilliance of particular works. We get the sense of a strong sure inward knowledge of the prospects of life and of his own life in the world, but also of an increasing diffidence or cursoriness in the gestures expressing this knowledge. The highest flight of eloquence in *Pierre* is, prophetically, on the Carlylean theme of the necessity of Silence, and the later stages of the novel are overrun with observations on the essential "namelessness" or "unspeakableness" of what lies deepest in existence. It is an awkward point of arrival for a writer who had thus far been committed to completeness and explicitness of statement as the true earnest of literary virtue.

Through the writing of *Pierre* the pace and momentum of Melville's career seem to change, to augment, almost month by month. Abruptly thereafter a different cycle begins. We are never again to get from his writing that impression of expansiveness and superfluent energy which all his earlier books deliver. The letters surviving from the summer and fall of 1852 show a tiredness and even apathy, at the least a reserve, which are suddenly prophetic of the remaining forty years of his life. As against his excited response to *The House of the Seven Gables,* in mid-April of 1851, a letter to Hawthorne acknowledging *The Blithedale Romance* (July 17, 1852) is noticeably perfunctory, though it is not cool or personally indifferent; the will toward friendship and the habit of bold declaration still assert themselves, but mechanically, without force of spirit. Later in the summer he wrote Hawthorne the long "Agatha" letter, offering the use, as lying closer to his friend's proven vein than to his own, of the emblematical story of a deserted New Bedford wife. It is a subdued letter; clearly Melville was in no state, five months after finishing *Pierre,* to undertake another book. Yet his imagination rises spontaneously enough to the subject, generating pictures, incidents, poignant openings for his own characteristic manner of meditative exposition. Two months later he was still considering the project, and still trying to get Hawthorne interested in it. In November he visited Hawthorne in Concord and at the latter's urging agreed, without much enthusiasm, to take it up himself—and that is the last we hear of it.[7] The rush of his mind's unfolding appears to be at an end. The pressure of his ambition to bear his witness no longer shows the presumptuous insistence of his years of growth. We may doubt that we are much the poorer because Melville did not, apparently, make a novel of "Agatha." The basic situation as he describes it is static, actionless; and it is questionable whether without the benefit of a rounded fable, such as he had the next year in "Bartleby," or of the personal recollection he could draw upon for "The Encantadas," or of the vitally personal subject that had engrossed him in the otherwise chaotic *Pierre,* he could have brought off those searching inferences and intimations that would have made the raw story worth his telling.

Melville's work up through *Pierre,* I have been trying to show, requires us to keep his own inward development directly in mind. This is not so for the work that remained. All his books up to this point had been conspicuously original in performance, and unrepetitive in presentation, but it was a kind of originality which now seemed to Melville mostly accidental

[7] On the question of what Melville may have written during the winter of 1852–1853, see *Letters of Herman Melville,* ed. Merrell R. Davis and William H. Gilman (New Haven, 1960), p. 164, footnotes 6 and 7. The "new work" said to be "nearly ready for the press" in April 1853 could conceivably have been the "Agatha" story, as the editors suggest; but there is at least as much reason to suspect that it was "Bartleby the Scrivener," carried by *Putnam's* in November and December of 1853, or else "Cock-a-Doodle-Doo!" which *Harper's New Monthly* printed in December 1853—especially if we relate it, as Davis and Gilman do, to the "work which I took to New York last spring, but which I was prevented from printing at that time" mentioned in Melville's letter to Harper Brothers of November 24, 1853. Unless new letters or manuscripts turn up, this important interval in Melville's life must remain obscure. But there seems little doubt that it encompassed a decisive alteration in his practice as a writer.

and which he was less and less inclined to prize. He appears to have had his own books in mind when he wrote, in *Pierre*, of how, "in the inferior instances of an immediate literary success, in very young writers, it will be almost invariably observable, that for that instant success they were chiefly indebted to some rich and peculiar experience in life, embodied in a book, which because, for that cause, containing original matter, the author himself, forsooth, is to be considered original; in this way, many very original books, being the product of very unoriginal minds." Of personal originality—and in the Romantic manner he meant something more than mere novelty—he now professed to despair as a writer. "The world is forever babbling of originality; but there never yet was an original man, in the sense intended by the world . . . the only original author being God." And the true voice of God, he asserted elsewhere in *Pierre*, is Silence. But perhaps the first thing to be emphasized in his work from 1853 to 1856 is just its originality, its actual freshness and variety of execution. No part of it approaches the magnitude of *Moby-Dick*, but the difference is of scale rather than of quality and kind; the best of it has, in its own way, a comparable authority. Yet in this one respect there is a radical difference—none of it openly calls attention, as does every one of his first seven books, to the personal presence of the writer, and very little of it strikes us as *primarily* testimonial or confessional.

In these later and mostly shorter writings we find Melville for the first time willingly confining his utterance within conventional forms, like the tale, the descriptive sketch, the familiar or fanciful essay; the forms, that is, favored by the magazine-public of the day. The work of these years is less "organic," less fused with private interrogation and self-consciousness, though it is not a bit less expressive of the consistent core of Melville's apprehension. And for the very reason that it is less revealing personally, it may actually be *more* instructive as art, more directly exemplary of the possibilities of imaginative composition. If Melville can serve as a practical model, it is likely to be in these performances. In a way the example presented by the creation of *Moby-Dick* is finally unapproachable. It is of a particular mind risking (through congenial forms yet very singular materials) the complete expenditure of its accessible resources and energies, and in the act forcing access even deeper—out of a heady confidence that the resources and energies are absolute and inexhaustible. But that confidence is itself a part of the energy, and integral to its release, and it is to that degree accidental and personal; we can only be amazed that it existed and that it pretty well held up through the writing of the book. The example Melville presents in his work after 1852, on the other hand, is of a mind still willing to risk expressing itself and its knowledge, still powerfully assertive once arrived at the point of speaking out, but husbanding its opportunities and formally disciplining its reserves of vitality. It has grown wary of the naked attack upon unspeakable truths. After *Pierre*, as Yvor Winters has put it, Melville writes consistently in the ordinary style of efficient prose. He is henceforth essentially explanatory of what he has to show, rather than rhapsodically or prophetically interjective of what he is in process of discovering.

I am going to risk laboring somewhat this point about Melville's career, for it seems to me fundamental. The question is of his performance as a writer. The growth and development that count for him as a writer—including the retrenchment and consolidation of performance first signalized in "Bartleby" and "Cock-a-Doodle-Doo!"—are over by 1853. His private trials of spirit were, of course, far from finished. His almost disabling obsession with first and last questions was really just beginning. Almost all the reports we have both about Melville's endless pursuit of "everything that lies beyond human ken" (as Hawthorne described it), and about his uncertain health and nervous instability, are from after 1852: Maunsell Field's account of his "brilliant" dialogue with Dr. Holmes on eastern religions; Evert

Duyckinck's of his being "charged to the muzzle with his sailor metaphysics and jargon of things unknowable"; Hawthorne's of the meeting in Liverpool in 1856, with Melville "much overshadowed since I saw him last" and stoically resolved to accept being "annihilated" but "too honest and courageous" to give up the search for truth; Henry Gansevoort's of his misanthropically "captious" conversation; a Williams College student's of an uninterruptible monologue of embittered philosophizing; the family letters concerning the urgency of his need for rest and recuperation. Before 1852, however, reports of Melville's manner and behavior have quite a different emphasis; we hear of his extravagant mimetic energy in telling stories, his power of vividly recreating the actual scenes and characters of his adventures, his way of raising ultimate questions about Truth and Being quite offhandedly, like any topic of common observation. Our problem is distinguishing the career of the writer from the personal history of the man; too often Melville's earlier books are interpreted as though composed to illustrate the later drift of his thought and feeling. But it was while his imaginative confidence and ambition were running strong and his energies were unimpaired that his work was so freely confessional and exploratory; and it is as his personal confidence seriously falters and "metaphysical" doubts rise up that his writing takes on, as though in self-defense, the formal constraint and strictness of demonstration that characterize nearly everything he put into print after *Pierre*.

Not that the subjects of these later prose pieces do not have a personal bearing. We observe how many in one way or another set before us the sequence of a whole life, and most often of a life which after adventuresome beginnings has trailed off into obscurity, desolation, inertness, or at best into humble or whimsical resignation. "Bartleby," "Cock-a-Doodle-Doo!" *Israel Potter*, "The Encantadas," "The Happy Failure," "The Fiddler," "The Bell-Tower," "Jimmy Rose," even "Benito Cereno" and "I and My Chimney," as well as certain stories told within

The Confidence-Man—all give us versions of this melancholy action, which is taken up again, later on, in Melville's poetry and in fragments like the admirable sketch of John Marr. More significant than the choice of subjects, though, is the performance, the high level of craftsmanship apparent through all this magazine-work. Under such disciplining the irrepressible boldness of Melville's matured outlook positively thrives. Yet the formal logic of the story, as such, is not violated; there is no impatient forcing of the fictional occasion, for the sake of impromptu truth-telling. Such is the strictness now of his impulse to clarify and demonstrate, and (as E. M. Forster shrewdly remarked in the case of *Billy Budd*) so little self-regarding, that it seeks only to identify as exactly as it can the specific narrative objects it fastens on; and its choice of these objects is original, large-minded, and superbly tactful. In the best of this shorter work of the mid-1850's we find Melville in solid possession of just that "really *grasping* imagination" which, according to Henry James fifteen years later, would be the thing required for mastery of such specifically American materials as existed for high literature.[8] Not even in *Moby-Dick* had Melville exercised this faculty so steadily. The result, in a story like "Bartleby," is a clarity of exposition and a tonic firmness and finality of implication which, to my judgment, decisively surpass the painstaking but fundamentally insulated and unventuresome art James contrived, in stories like "The Bench of Desolation," for tracing out his own "American" images of wasted, self-ruined life.

These qualities in the writing nearly make up for the obvious faults of construction in Melville's two novels of this period, *Israel Potter* and *The Confidence-Man*, both of which give an impression of exceptional imaginative power scattering its effects more or less at random. Some admirers of *The Confidence-Man*

[8] James to C. E. Norton, January 16, 1871. The phrase is used to describe what seemed to be missing in Howells' otherwise admirable "American" realism.

find more organization in it than I can; some even make out a coherent allegorical design. What I should prefer to stress is the book's almost haphazard imaginative consistency. Composed in different personal circumstances, it might indeed have been a masterpiece, of scarcely less authority than *Moby-Dick.* Even as it stands, it seems positively to anticipate the manner of certain classics of early twentieth-century fiction. Incomplete but coherent, dense in detail, static in conception, single-mindedly mimicking certain conspicuous norms of modern civilized behavior, it calls to mind such admirable books as Svevo's *Confessions of Zeno* or Silone's *Seed Beneath the Snow,* and is just as tiring to get through; for in ringing the changes on the metaphor of "confidence," it so thoroughly, moment by moment, delivers itself of its whole subject and point of view that the most approving reader can take in hardly more than twenty pages at a time. Like these later novels, it is a work organized by the repetitions of one simple modal action,[9] and correspondingly by the rhythmic assertions of a single sustaining perspective. This perspective, in *The Confidence-Man,* is at once moral and exegetical. It judges and it denominates; it is both satirical and anatomizing. We test its authenticity by the consistency of the address, by style. We test its importance, however, by the catholicity of its reach, and we find not only that it spans a broad range of occasions and concerns, but that it is formally creative of new occasions and analogous further concerns. With a vividness of emphasis that seems, as we observe it, to surprise life itself, the thrust of imagination in *The Confidence-Man* creates—according to the angle and mass of its local attack—the very scenes it so solidly particularizes. It is not finally a good *novel,* but it is an altogether extraordinary exercise of creative imagination, and an absorbing book.

[9] I.e., the dehumanizing, virtue-corrupting intercourse of persons in a society, a world, that by an absolute unquestioning conspiracy appears to have substituted the convenient, one-to-one, self-interest-serving, bargained relationship, as flimsy and treacherous as the words it is cast in, for every natural form of human co-existence.

V

With *The Confidence-Man* Melville's public career as a writer of stories abruptly breaks off. Of his later life little need be said here. Mrs. Metcalf's documentary volume presents its fluctuations and slow withdrawal sensitively and in sufficient detail. Perhaps a later writer, or one coming more deliberately and knowledgeably into his career, would have been better prepared for the alienation, not only from popular approval but more significantly from his own vocation, that overtook Melville; but he was Baudelaire's exact contemporary, and thus of the first generation to experience as a matter of course this now familiar and much-advertised condition of existence for the imaginative artist. Also it is to be kept in mind that he was, after all, unique among the major American talents of his time in having been able to bring to his most ambitious work the encouragement of a breakaway popular success; otherwise, we can well imagine, he might never have executed it at all. After 1856, thrown back upon himself for incentive and approbation, he produced chiefly fragments (*Clarel* is the exception, and writing it, in an alien form, nearly wrecked him). But these fragments, though incomplete and inharmonious in themselves, are all broken off the same falling mass, and are all expressive of an absorbing inward drama of personal endurance. All, too, are mimetic of the rare personal integrity of a singularly liberal and responsive mind, and speak in their various odd ways for certain constant mysteries of human virtue.

Through this long time of disability, withdrawal, and resignation, two intuitions appear to hold relatively firm, and even to find renewal. One is of the possibility of nobleness in "some men," of "character picturesquely great" (to take a phrase from "The Marquis de Grandvin"); the other, of an undying beauty of youthfulness in the heart of mankind as in the "weeds and wildings" at the heart of nature. Both, we observe, are expressly realized in *Billy Budd*. A certain simplification of judgment and concern gradually interceded. "One gets to care less and less," Melville wrote his brother-in-law, John Hoadley, a year after *Clarel*, "for everything except downright good feeling. Life is so short, and so ridiculous and irrational (from a certain point of view). . . ." So in "John Marr" we are shown a desolating picture of a way of life which, though decently industrious and self-respecting, is without this one redeeming quality, this "geniality, the flower of life, springing from some sense of joy in it, more or less." Elsewhere among the poems we come upon a series of figures (the Marquis de Grandvin and Major Jack Gentian, Bridegroom Dick, Jack Roy, the meditative old "rose farmer") who embody a certain courteous, worldly geniality, neither cynical nor weakly sentimental, but full of practical charity and sympathy. "There is no mortal sin," one of his last and tidiest poems declares—"No, none to us but Malice!" The apprehension of tragedy, of moral deformity and personal disaster, remained unabated, as *Billy Budd* magnificently reminds us. But what Melville had written at the end of the Civil War in the prose "Supplement" to his *Battle-Pieces*, in declining to raise his voice polemically against the grave dangers of an oppressive peace, speaks as well for the state of mind—the anguished awareness, the corresponding reserve—of all his declining years: "But this path of thought leads toward those waters of bitterness from which one can only turn aside and be silent."

CHAPTER THREE

THE MELVILLEAN SETTING

"Things must be accepted as they are. It is not for nothing that all the great novels we now like best are a bit heavy. The poet may set forth, a wandering minstrel, with his lyre under his arm, but the novelist moves with cumbrous baggage like circuses or nomadic tribes. He carries the furnishings of a whole world on his back."—ORTEGA, "Notes on the Novel"

". . . the creative consciousness of the order of existence."—JOHN SLOAN, *Gist of Art*

MELVILLE'S first readers, trying to define their delight in the unheralded *Typee,* mainly stressed the book's pictorial merits, its descriptive charm and vivacity. In so doing they recognized, in effect, the kind of public acceptance it was bidding for, among such commodities of the nineteenth-century popular market as the romantic "traveler's tale" and various other more or less exotic types of landscape and genre sketchwork. A "Frenchy coloured picture of the Marquesan islanders" is how Evert Duyckinck privately characterized *Typee,* while Margaret Fuller, a critic of rather different persuasions, commended it for its "pretty and spirited pictures." Certain reviewers, however, in granting these pictures the further quality of "verisimilitude," intimated a weightier reason for respecting the author's accomplishment. Evidently the book's romantic picturesqueness was not incompatible with a convincing particularity and definiteness of delineation. Melville himself had claimed in the preface that his narrative was "based upon facts" and that it presented "the unvarnished truth"; and while such claims were usual for such work, yet we may observe that though the narrator's adventures were widely questioned as to their authenticity, his descriptions and scenic effects were not. "A little colouring there may be, here and there," one cautious reviewer commented, "but the result is a thorough impression of reality." The impressive veracity of the Melvillean scene is something, it seems, to be reckoned with from the start.

What were Melville's chances with the conventions he took up at this inadvertent outset of his career? The fashion of the picturesque, the romantic taste for pleasures of landscape and scene, may be said to derive at some point from a consciousness (justified or not) of the economic mastery of nature and the physical world. That fashion and taste seem characteristic of much western art, though not usually the best of it, during the past two or three hundred years of progress in social comfort and material convenience; they seem characteristic, too, of the leisure-class sensibility upon which this art has increasingly depended for patronage. The contemplative, passively appreciative attitude of observation adopted by the connoisseur of scenic patterns and prospects speaks for the broadening personal security allowed by the modern bourgeois order of life to its privileged classes (anxieties aside), with its grant of immunity from the immediate struggle with natural conditions. So one is free to admire or to relish what scenes one finds oneself free to come and go among, what has clearly been subdued by the expropriating advance of civilization, what no longer in any given place has to be taken as the whole decisive environment of economic occupation. No wonder then that scenic description in literature—including more recently the *paysage* of industrialism and the city—runs as much risk of complacency and insipidness as anecdotal painting or program music; and no wonder that moralists of style as various as Stendhal, Keats, Flaubert, Dr. Johnson, and Ezra Pound should all have spoken out against it.[1]

[1] With respect to aesthetic theory, the whole question of description in the arts, and of such concepts as the picturesque, the sublime, the beauti-

Yet an interest in landscape as such, and our ordinary patience with mere description and observation (as with mere anecdote in conversation or the newspapers), are legitimate in their own way. They stem from a proper curiosity about the composed order of the things of this world. They reveal, too, a multiplying need to fill up the multiplying emptinesses in the adult conditioning our society ordinarily offers. (Poe, in a sketch like "The Domain of Arnheim," calculatingly appealed to motives of this sort, more especially to the parvenu insecurity of his magazine audience and its peculiar anxiety about correctness of taste, by working out in terms of landscape a quasi-spiritual fantasy of material perfection, in which the susceptible eye of man would be marvelously soothed and even encouraged to think itself immortal.) The point is that the potential value of such curiosity and such need is not diminished by the usual shabbiness of the articles produced to satisfy them. Given a producer with some respect for the measure of reality, the popular fashion can be made to yield sound and durable work—a painter, for example, interested in the whole structure and life-cycle of phenomenal objects and not only in his diffused sensation of them; or a writer equipped to discover within the scene in view the hieroglyph, so to speak, of its essential organization, and thus to render it according to the whole aspect of its human and civil uses.

ful, and the imitation of nature, is extremely complicated, and has been very carefully investigated in modern scholarship. I hope I may be excused from raising it here—as I should surely have had to in discussing the work of a graphic artist. Even then, however, the argument might finally have turned on historical considerations. I would agree with Malraux that in the history of painting the studied concern for the exact appearances of things, from the point of view of the individual observer, was a relatively short-term aberration, expressing the historical cresting of that confident, rationalized, individualistic humanism (or false humanism) which history itself in due course has rather savagely given the lie to. Perhaps more or less the same thing may be said of the philosophies of perception and cognition that provided this concern with an aesthetic rationale. To assume that the significant, apprehensible world is identical with the visible scene is indeed to lie about it, to pass it off as a good deal less than in operation it actually is, to ready it for whatever kind of exploitation one has in mind.

For what most interests us in landscape are the signs of human occupation, and all the evidences of the tension (resolved this way or that, and subject to infinite complication) between physical nature and human economy. No part of the known, encountered world is without its traceable history in this respect.[2] And is there anything, it may be asked, more worth discovering, among the things it is possible to discover, than the design of this history? Is not an understanding of it the fundamental justification of humane learning, and a proper culmination of our otherwise pitiful self-knowledge? To get at it, we feel, the writer has only to extend his powers of attentiveness and perseverance, and that capacity for straight impressions that Henry James spoke up for (I do not mean not to stand in some awe of these rare virtues); in any event it is not his materials that will fail him.

For such a writer the business of appeasing his readers' ordinary curiosity by means of vivid description may turn out to be a providential source of creative renewal. It may, for instance, open a way of escaping the idolatry of *person* and *self* into which "modern" literature, despite the labors of its chief craftsmen, is still sinking. If by description it is possible to project the determining conditions, or the signs of them, which support the ways of life that pass current, then the account of those ways of life, in whatever mode, may be restored to importance, to serious interest. And if these determining conditions are conceived in anything like their proper magnitude and actual complexity and energy, then a true account of the experience

[2] Except perhaps its untenanted extremities: polar wastes, 8,000-meter peaks, rain forests, deserts, or outposts like the Galapagos Islands, which became Melville's extraordinary Encantadas. And except the sea. But these all have, of course, their human relevance. Melville himself discovered what any expedition-chronicler must learn, that such places are made most impressive, most precisely imaginable, by the truthful detailing of what exactly is required of human beings to survive there. No adjectival rhapsody can suggest so well their actual wildness and strangeness. What they are, moreover, all the earth was once—unpeopled, unmarked by man, indifferent to his ingenious colonizing.

of them will correspond in some measure, and a literature of moral weight and moment becomes possible again; its heroes will not be the less heroic, nor the actions it displays the less impressive, because they are shown to be required (even absolutely) by the discovered necessities of the scene.[3] Melville found all this out as he worked—and that is one great reason why for all its hurry and formal roughness his writing, which is so heavily descriptive and explanatory, so strongly endures. In this respect his work is visionary, like that of all the great masters of descriptive expression. His own most splendid heroes rise most vividly to his imagination dressed in the physical stuff and circumstance of their occupations, and of them he learned to say: "Not so much thy skill then, O hunter, as the great necessities that strike thy victory to thee" (*Moby-Dick*, Chapter 85). The great scenes in his narratives come alive precisely through the transmitted apprehension, in full material detail, of these "great necessities," the sum of which composes the determining setting for the events being shown.

Even in the raw picturesqueness of *Typee* Melville is more than simply a "graphic" writer. His early books are in fact rather less thoroughgoing descriptively than, say, Dana's solid and conscientious *Two Years Before the Mast* (1840). He scants as much as he gives, in the way of observed fact. But you do not get from Dana's book that impression which one contemporary reviewer made a special point of attributing to the writing in *Omoo:* the impression of an imaginative power in reserve, a romance-making power "of prolonging these adventures to any extent for which a public may demand them." What Melville's imagination has broken through to, as Dana's Harvard decorum never could, is the knockabout comedy of his own participation in what he is describing. (This in turn provides a basis in

[3] See George D. Painter's presentation, in *Proust: The Early Years* (London, 1959), of Proust's great novel as essentially, in form, a descriptive interpretation of reality.

ordinary incident for pointing up, as Melville now and then remembers to do, certain significant contrasts between Polynesian and Anglo-Saxon civilization.) In *Omoo,* in fact, the adventuring becomes dominant and largely displaces the picture-making—the result being that raffish, occasionally rather callow chronicle of island-scrounging and gold-bricking in which D. H. Lawrence, for one, found Melville at his happiest. What one most remembers of this sequel to *Typee* are neither the pictorial effects nor the blunt observations on the disaster to Tahitian society of western influence, but certain odd bits of social comedy revealing the local customs and hand-to-mouth economics of this matter-of-factly rendered, half-caste sub-civilization—the Calabooza and the Broom Road; Shorty's and Zeke's potato plantation; and various grotesque or pathetic details of what our own era, with chilling irony, has chosen to call "fraternization." *Omoo* stays in the mind more distinctly than *Typee* and *Mardi,* I think, precisely as it does constitute a practical handbook in how to make a living in the world without actually working (in an environment so ridiculously hospitable that the account of getting along in it becomes a kind of travesty on a commercial society's rigorous conceptions of the struggle for existence). By contrast the archipelago setting or "world" of *Mardi,* though more assiduously worked up, fails to be as impressive, being coordinated through allegorical abstractions and not by any consistent observation of day-to-day life; no one is naturally on the job in its wholly idealized landscape.

It appears that Melville's genius for description and scene-painting required, as with any serious writer, its validating human occasions. But in this respect he was not restricted to his personal fund of adventure. Two works most notable for scene and atmosphere, and most expertly pictorial, are *Israel Potter* and "Benito Cereno," and both of these were in good part pieced together out of old documents, the main substance of which Melville somewhat reinterpreted but did not systematically change. The simple progression of both these narratives is that of a series of pictures. It is not really the action, or the often rather clumsy presentation of the action, that page by page organizes their special effects, but the succession of mood-asserting tableaux the action leads into—though these are of course dependent on the action's going plausibly forward. Something not very different may be said in fact of the organization of *Moby-Dick*, the whole of which is built up along certain constant relations between the action and its copiously elaborated setting. The stage of *Moby-Dick*, Edwin Muir remarked, is vast but it is also unchanging; it is literally world-wide, but "all the exits are closed." It is also marvelously and voluminously double—there is the great oceanic globe, of a grandeur appropriate to the drama of the titanic hero; but there is also the ship, that wholly self-contained factory and theater of human occupations, by means of which, as it gets patiently and exhaustively described through the circuit of the narrative, Melville gives physical body and truth to his fantastic story.

In all these works the effective setting is something more than the sum of background (or foreground) descriptions. It embraces also the kinds of life and enterprise that are proper to the conditions presented, and it includes some corresponding view of the capacity for action and reaction within the human agent. It realizes, that is, a general view of nature and a general view of human nature. I am convinced that there is no simpler way of defining *setting*, in Melville's case.

II

Israel Potter (1854–1855) is an odd item in the Melville canon. The one book of his to be serialized in magazine form, running for nine months in *Putnam's*, it bears the marks of this method of composition, being impromptu to the point of negligence in its narrative sequence and correspondingly erratic in emphasis and detail. It contains, however, a succession of individual scenes that stand out sharply from the rather casual order of their occurrence. The story seems to have been undertaken as a piece of job-work—Melville had picked up a rare copy of the *Life and Remarkable Adventures of Israel R. Potter* in 1849, the year of "beggarly" *Redburn* and *White-Jacket*—and the unevenness of his performance in it is a little exasperating. Newton Arvin accurately remarks of it that it "might conceivably have been a superb book," but is in fact no more than "a heap of sketches . . . for a masterpiece that never got composed." The appeal to Melville's imagination of Israel Potter's story—through a life of exile, heroic and secretive adventure, poverty, and oblivion—is not hard to understand. But in the book as we have it, that story is only outlined. The novel, if it may be called that, makes its impression instead as a series of preparatory sketches of scene and background: the night meeting of American conspirators in Paris, the desert wilderness of London and Israel's several approaches to it, the shorescapes of Whitehaven and Flamborough Head, the purgatorial brickyard where Israel labors, and so on. It stands thus as a compilation of vividly circumstantial settings for a life-history which, however, was so much determined by circumstance and setting that to summon *them* up exhausted such interest as *it* might have possessed in itself. There are vigorous incidental portraits, as of Franklin and John Paul Jones. But the figure of Israel remains indistinct. The full course of his life comes to seem as much of an "hallucination" to us as his memories of it eventually are to him. What we do finally know of its design and its meaning derives mainly from the intimations of general human destiny that are delivered to us from time to time in the exposition of these preparatory scenes.

One such passage of exposition makes up the whole first chapter of the narrative, and to give a specific instance of Melville's descriptive style I shall quote here the greater part of it. A perfunctory opening paragraph launches "the traveller" into the "singular scenery" of the isolated western Massachusetts up-country where Israel was born, a region lying out of the way of the "general tourist" but providing, we are told, "ample food for poetic reflection." Out of this commonplace introduction the main passage now develops:

"Travelling northward from the township of Otis, the road leads for twenty or thirty miles towards Windsor, lengthwise upon that long broken spur of heights which the Green Mountains of Vermont send into Massachusetts. For nearly the whole of the distance, you have the continual sensation of being upon some terrace in the moon. The feeling of the plain or valley is never yours; scarcely the feeling of the earth. Unless by a sudden precipitation of the road you find yourself plunging into some gorge, you pass on, and on, and on, upon the crests or slopes of pastoral mountains, while far below, mapped out in its beauty, the valley of the Housatonic lies endlessly along at your feet. Often, as your horse gaining some lofty level tract, flat as a table, trots gayly over the almost deserted and sodded road, and your admiring eye sweeps the broad landscape beneath, you seem to be Boótes driving in heaven. Save a potato field here and there, at long intervals, the whole country is either in wood or pasture. Horses, cattle and sheep are the principal inhabitants of these mountains. But all through the year lazy columns of smoke, rising from the depths of the forest, proclaim the presence of that half-outlaw, the charcoal-burner; while in early spring added curls of vapor show that the maple sugar-boiler is also at work. But as for farming as a regular vocation, there is not much of it here. At any rate, no man by that means accumulates a fortune from this thin and rocky soil, all whose arable parts have long since been nearly exhausted.

"Yet during the first settlement of the country, the region was not unproductive. Here it was that the original settlers came, acting upon the principle well known to have regulated their choice of site, namely, the high land in preference to the low, as less subject to the unwholesome miasmas generated by breaking into the rich valleys and alluvial bottoms of primeval regions. By degrees, however, they quitted the safety of this sterile elevation, to brave the dangers of richer though lower fields. So that, at the present day, some of those mountain townships present an aspect of singular abandonment. Though they have never known aught but peace and health, they, in one lesser aspect at least, look like countries depopulated by plague and war. Every mile or two a house is passed untenanted. The strength of the frame-work of these ancient buildings enables them long to resist the encroachments of decay. Spotted gray and green with the weather-stain, their timbers seem to have lapsed back into their woodland original, forming part now of the general picturesqueness of the natural scene. They are of extraordinary size, compared with modern farmhouses. One peculiar feature is the immense chimney, of light gray stone, perforating the middle of the roof like a tower.

"On all sides are seen the tokens of ancient industry. As stone abounds throughout these mountains, that material was, for fences, as ready to the hand as wood, besides being much more durable. Consequently the landscape is intersected in all directions with walls of uncommon neatness and strength.

"The number and length of these walls is not more surprising than the size of some of the blocks comprising them. The very Titans seemed to have been at work. That so small an army as the first settlers must needs have been, should have taken such wonderful pains to enclose so ungrateful a soil; that they should have accomplished such herculean undertakings with so slight a prospect of reward; this is a consideration which gives us a significant hint of the temper of the men of the Revolutionary era.

"Nor could a fitter country be found for the birthplace of the devoted patriot, Israel Potter.

"To this day the best stone-wall builders, as the best woodchoppers, come from those solitary mountain towns; a tall, athletic, and hardy race, unerring with the axe as the Indian with the tomahawk; at stone-rolling, patient as Sisyphus, powerful as Samson."

Two long paragraphs of descriptive evocation follow, the first detailing the pleasures of summer in these upland districts—grassy meadows, light winds, great spaces—when natural beauty so "populates the loneliness" that "you would not have the country more settled if you could," the second reinforcing this note with an account of the birds of the region in their summer flights and singing. Then the major theme, abandonment and isolation, is resumed:

"But in autumn, those gay northerners, the birds, return to their southern plantations. The mountains are left bleak and sere. Solitude settles down upon them in drizzling mists. The traveller is beset, at perilous turns, by dense masses of fog. He emerges for a moment into more penetrable air; and passing some gray, abandoned house, sees the lofty vapors plainly eddy by its desolate door; just as from the plain you may see it eddy by the pinnacles of distant and lonely heights. Or, dismounting from his frightened horse, he leads him down some scowling glen, where the road steeply dips among grim rocks, only to rise as abruptly again; and as he warily picks his way, uneasy at the menacing scene, he sees some ghost-like object looming through the mist at the roadside; and wending towards it, beholds a rude white stone, uncouthly inscribed, marking the spot where, some fifty or sixty years ago, some farmer was upset in his woodsled, and perished beneath the load.

"In winter this region is blocked up with snow. Inaccessible and impassable, those wild, unfrequented roads, which in August are overgrown with high grass, in December are drifted to the arm-pit with the white fleece from the sky. As if an ocean rolled between man and man, intercommunication is often suspended for weeks and weeks.

"Such, at this day, is the country which gave birth to our hero. . . ."

What exactly is achieved in this passage? It is a good example, for one thing, of an aspect of Melville's writing previously mentioned—its way of capitalizing on its own (often precarious) forward momentum, and devising an effective form and address out of its own first casual improvisations. In the gathering consistency and sureness of the observation, a power of implication is built up that can be turned to account; here, for example, it releases a phrase which is as simple and factual as the rest of the description, yet which operates as both a climax and a portent ("As if an ocean rolled between man and man . . ."). The passage also gives us specific intimations of the whole story to follow: the herculean labor of the vanished settlers prefigures the sturdy "western" heroics of Paul Jones and Ethan Allen, and the progression of seasons into bleak winter anticipates the melancholy changes of Israel's life. But what I want to stress here is simply the immediate interest of this opening passage, taken by itself. What a capable writer is modestly at work in it, and how much more than a mere purveyor of the picturesque and romantic! And what an uncommonly interesting book might develop from it. By plain observation, precise yet freely inventive in pursuing semblances and allusions, and by the steadily tactful placing of epithet and detail, the scene is both composed and interpreted, so that out of its concordant appearances there gradually emerges a large, whole image of an entire region in the vivid natural cycle of its occupancy by men. Through the variety of the facts presented and through the depth in time and social usage of their imagined lodgment, we have in fact been brought forward into the major sphere of narrative fiction, the sphere of the collective and historical, of folk-recollection and of legend. The ground has been prepared for a story with all the authority of myth—though it is only negligently cultivated in what follows. If Melville did indeed possess the myth-making faculty of imagination that criticism has claimed for him, it is surely as apparent here as in his more deliberately emblematic writing.

This setting tells us much of what the life of the character born into it will tell us, but does so in its own sufficient terms. It is not merely a foretelling. Not to see this is really to miss, I think, the characteristic strength of Melville's creative intelligence. It is interesting to compare this passage from *Israel Potter* with Hawthorne's rendering of the same Berkshire landscape in the "chapter from an abortive romance" which he called "Ethan Brand"; for what is missing from Hawthorne's expert but static fable of exile and nemesis—and, it might be said, from his several in some degree abortive attempts to bring off a satisfactory novel after *The Scarlet Letter*—is this kind of summary yet concrete and realistic conception of the collective history that operates through individual lives. We may imagine how such a conception might have made the setting of "Ethan Brand" something more than a projection of the protagonist's spiritual state, and how it might in general have given body and footing to Hawthorne's rare and exact concern for the "deeper psychology" (as Henry James put it), "the whole deep mystery of man's soul and conscience." Melville's mature work is scarcely less fanciful or fable-prone than Hawthorne's, but it does not so commonly require the exemptions of "romance." Its legends are not primarily of the soul, but of the common existence of men in the constituted world. It expresses perhaps an even rarer concern in American writing, a concern, we might call it, borrowing the Jamesian cadence, for the deeper biography. Thus it combines, as here in *Israel Potter*, the intuitions concerning the life of the soul characteristic of a Hawthorne, a Poe, an Emily Dickinson, with the feeling for collective destinies that distinguishes a Cooper or a Henry Adams—or, as it happens, a Tocqueville, who had earlier used this image of ruins sinking back into the returning wilderness to symbolize the ambiguous "progress of man" in the circumstance of the new world.[4]

What I would suggest here about the ground of interest in Melville's descriptive writing is borne out, somewhat paradoxically perhaps, in the beautiful "Encantadas" sequence. All through these vivid "sketches," as they are labeled, weird graphic details of the barren wasteland of the Galapagos Islands are emphasized in a manner that seems appropriate to the pseudonym of "Salvator R. Tarnmoor" under which the work was first published (in *Putnam's*, March–May 1854). That pseudonym, however, is misleading, and was in fact discarded when the sketches were reprinted in *Piazza Tales* two years later. Once again the romantic picturesque is, for Melville, only a means to a more serious end. From the short opening paragraph of the first sketch, with its laconic reference to cinder heaps on the edge of some modern city and its abrupt terminal vision of "the world at large . . . after a penal conflagration," the disguise of landscape romanticism is quickly put aside and the characteristically Melvillean point of view is asserted.

The first and strongest note sounded in "The Encantadas" is the absence of any but the most transient, futile, and desperate marks of human occupation. On most of these islands physical nature has not yielded an inch to the progress of man; they are islands "without history." To them, "change never comes"—and that is their special curse. The only indigenous creatures are reptiles and spiders; "the chief sound of life here is a hiss." But we observe quickly enough that Melville has made all this desolation concrete and poignant precisely by the

[4] *Democracy in America,* I, xvii: "Accidental or Providential Causes which contribute to maintain the Democratic Republic in the United States."

There is another such passage in Melville's Civil War poem, "The Scout toward Aldie" (stanzas 21–24), in which a "spell-bound" landscape of abandoned farms and crossroads, overgrown with vegetation, is the setting for the ghostly forays of Mosby's raiders.

measure of human association: by an emphasis on what is absent, by the starkness of the differences from the familiar settled world, by certain tales told of those "runaways, castaways, and solitaries" who from time to time have happened ashore. The islands may be without inhabitants or history, but they are not without names—"Jervis Isle, Duncan Isle, Crossman's Isle, Brattle Isle, Wood's Isle, Chatham Isle," and so on—the marvelous unforgettable names of men, assigned by their unabashed discoverers and navigators. The Encantadas are presented as an "other and darker" world than ours, yet as grimly a part of ours as well, for "in no world but a fallen one could such lands exist." A place of "penal hopelessness," they serve only to provide bitter "asylum" for refugees and derelicts from the outer world. So also, to their dead shores, "decayed bits of sugar-cane, bamboos, and cocoanuts" come drifting in, having floated there "from the charming palm isles to the westward and southward; all the way from Paradise to Tartarus," and along with these, even more ominously, "fragments of charred wood and moldering ribs of wrecks."

It is the severity of this reiterated contrast to the established civil world, and the concreteness and consistency of the emblems chosen to define it, that provide in "The Encantadas" the formal basis for the whole effort of description. As in the second sketch, on the "antediluvian-looking" tortoises, Melville can play easily back and forth between very different tones—awe and jocularity, gravity and grotesque fancifulness—without losing imaginative control. The writing, with this bold and simple opposition to illustrate, is solidly yet easily informative. The sentences, whether describing objects or the mind's reaction to objects, are full of plain facts. "The Encantadas," we might say, moves to some of the finest English prose in nineteenth-century literature by being, first of all, admirably efficient journalism.

III

Of all Melville's work it was *Moby-Dick* which, in its magnitude and boldness of design, laid the heaviest tribute upon his descriptive powers, and most strenuously tested his ambition to seek out the deeper logic of fact and appearance. It is of course his masterpiece. And one great factor in his accomplishment in *Moby-Dick* is the grandeur and animation of the settings, which in turn do not merely illustrate the book's action and themes but actively create them. The larger part of the narrative is simply the patiently detailed yet consistently high-spirited setting out of a scene sufficiently vast and prodigious to contain the central drama and justify its intensity. Melville's job is to create for us the huge "world" he means dramatically to exploit. This must be done, we are told at the end of Chapter 69, for perfectly practical reasons: a mass of particular facts must be faithfully explained so that when the climax comes we can follow its concentrated moments of action at their proper pace. But what is actually amassed in the long, richly digressive descriptive chronicle spun out by Ishmael is something more than we need for keeping track of the material events of the story. It is its own end and justification. The narrative, in the large, is nothing less than a confession *à fond* of the several "worlds" human existence marvelously moves through—and in this multiform context Ahab himself is in some danger of becoming only an incidental marvel, one among many, and a rather mechanical one at that. At a certain date in our acquaintance with the book *Moby-Dick* we are are no longer in doubt about the outcome; nor can we still be entirely surprised or astounded by the more highly wrought individual passages, of meditation, description, comedy, bravura declamation, analogy-running, or whatever, though we continue to be charmed by them. What does still lay claim on us then, and perhaps more powerfully than ever, is the imaginative coherence and embrace of the whole. The correspondences, the insistent illusion of a universe brimful of consenting and conspiring phenomena ceaselessly interacting, prove to be not forced but in the nature of the revealed materials. "Nothing exists in itself," Ishmael casually announces—a declaration which could seem rankest undergraduate sophistry, if it was not delivered, without emphasis, by someone who (starting in the first sentence of the first chapter with his own simple name) has proved himself able to call up and exactly identify so great a host of particular phenomena, of things as (to our eyes and in our hands) they actually are.

It should be evident that by "setting" I mean something more than the environment or material occasion within which the drama is played out. I mean rather that whole context, as the narrative establishes it, out of which the action rises—a context of idea and feeling as well as of observation and description; I mean all that in the convenient language of recent criticism may be called the "world" of behavior peculiar to an author's vision of existence. In *Moby-Dick* four distinct "worlds" may be defined, and all are fundamental to the import of the novel as Melville built it up.

(1) With the narrative beginning ashore and staying ashore for twenty-odd chapters, the first "world" put before us is that of the dry land, or at least the thronged edges of it: New York, New Bedford, Nantucket, and the streets, chapels, inns, and offices to be met on the way to the sea. It has its own solid attractions. There are chowder shops and good fellowship, there is the chance of fresh adventure, there is easy access to the earth's far corners and wildest wonders, and there is no shortage of incidental curiosities close at hand. In contrast to the Liverpool of *Redburn* or the New York of *Pierre* and "Bartleby," the cities and harbors of *Moby-Dick* seem hospitable places on the whole, and are presented with a good deal of homely charm and idealizing humor. But the land-world of this part of the book also supplies just as much motive as is needed for heading us willingly out into the "open independ-

ence of the sea." It is, successively, a dream-tormented world of unsatisfied yearnings, a "stepmother" world, a "wolfish" world, a world which "pays dividends" to sharp practice, a finished and unameliorable world of frost, death, teeth-chattering, and the sorrows of the orphaned, and of poverty and hard bargaining; a world finally (as even in the intensifying rush of the book's closing movement the figures of the carpenter and blacksmith do not let us forget) which is continually casting away the human wrecks and derelicts it has stripped and ruined.

(2) It is, in short, the world of men, whose "permanent constitutional condition," we are told, is "sordidness." The next broad context which the narrative begins to build up is also a world of men, but here Melville develops a different emphasis. For this is the self-sufficient world of the quaint, rare, old, noble, trophy-garnished, battle-worn, cannibalistic, melancholy *Pequod*; and Melville's purpose in describing it is to show it as a fit instrument for Ahab and his purpose and for all the "high and mighty business of whaling." The ship takes the center of the stage in Chapter 16, and continues to make a vividly heraldic presence throughout the rest of the book. Primarily a maneuverable slaughterhouse, as the narrative troubles to make spectacularly clear, she is at the same time, in the nature of her business of manufacturing oil, "among the cleanliest things of this tidy earth." Her high qualities are displayed in a series of brilliant and precise physical images: rushing after her boats in the first lowering, beating her way into the sleet and swell of Cape storms, gliding through yellow meadows of brit, pressing up the Sunda Strait in chase of an armada of whales and being chased in turn by armed pirates, and so on. As the concentrated foreground of the book's developing action, she has her own great part to play in it, and a series of descriptive epithets is used, in the manner of epic formulae, to point this up: so we hear of "the tranced ship," the "intense Pequod," "the

fated Pequod," "the madly merry and predestinated craft," and —perhaps most beautiful and foreboding of all—"the ivory Pequod."

Coincidentally the ship is shown to be a virtual city of the races and talents of men. From the first we are encouraged to think of her as a paradigm of the marvelous hive of corporate human life (though Melville does not impose that symbolism on the whole novel)—she is at once a parliament, guildhall, factory, and fortress, and goes "ballasted with utilities" like the world-renewing Ark itself. Different phases of the work that goes on aboard her and in her boats furnish metaphors for the different ways of "this world," as in chapters like "The Line" or "Fast Fish and Loose Fish." Mostly, however, the skills and practices of whaling are described for their own sake and in their own full detail, so that the fanciful analogies which are Melville's trademark in chapter-endings are usually erected on an already solid ground of factual interest. Indeed the long succession of passages describing the crew at its jobs makes up a "song for occupations" as comprehensive and ecstatic as Whitman's. Conversely we find Melville turning back to the general routine of common earthly labor for descriptive metaphors, invoking the whole range of its trades, tools, and artifacts in aid of his exposition. Such effects, we must agree, are wonderfully natural in *Moby-Dick*. For merely to describe one feature of the whale's anatomy or of the practical business of stripping it down is to give an impression of surveying no small part of the fantastic material apparatus by which ordinary civilized life is maintained. Consider the following:

"Let us now with whatever *levers* and *steam-engines* we have at hand, *cant over* the sperm whale's head, so that it may lie bottom up; then, ascending by a *ladder* to the summit, have a peep down the mouth; and were it not that the body is now completely separated from it, with a *lantern* we might descend into the great Kentucky Mammoth Cave of his stomach. But let us hold on here by this tooth, and look about us where we are. What a really beautiful and chaste-looking mouth! from *floor* to *ceiling*, lined, or rather *papered* with a glistening white membrane, glossy as *bridal satins*.

"But come out now, and look at this portentous lower jaw, which seems like the long narrow *lid* of an immense *snuff-box*, with the *hinge* at one end, instead of one side. If you *pry it up*, so as to get it overhead, and expose its rows of teeth, it seems a terrific *portcullis*; and such, alas! it proves to many a poor wight in the fishery, upon whom these *spikes* fall with *impaling* force. But far more terrible is it to behold, when fathoms down in the sea, you see some sulky whale, floating there suspended, with his prodigious jaw, some fifteen feet long, hanging straight down at right-angles with his body, for all the world like a *ship's jib-boom*. . . .

"In most cases this lower jaw—being easily *unhinged* by a practised artist—is disengaged and *hoisted* on deck for the purpose of extracting the ivory teeth, and furnishing a supply of that hard white whalebone with which the fishermen fashion *all sorts of curious articles, including canes, umbrella-stocks, and handles to riding-whips*.

"With a long, weary *hoist* the jaw is dragged on board, as if it were an *anchor*; and when the proper time comes—some few days after the other work—Queequeg, Daggoo, and Tashtego, being all *accomplished dentists*, are set to drawing teeth. With a keen *cutting-spade*, Queequeg *lances* the gums; then the jaw is *lashed down to ringbolts*, and *a tackle being rigged* from aloft, they drag out these teeth, *as Michigan oxen drag stumps of old oaks out of wild wood-lands*. There are generally forty-two teeth in all; in old whales, much worn down, but undecayed; *nor filled after our artificial fashion*. The jaw is afterwards *sawn into slabs*, and *piled away like joists for building houses*." [End of Chapter 74; italics mine, of course.]

This is not the sort of passage usually brought forward to make claims for *Moby-Dick*; yet only a writer of extraordinary attentiveness, and compassion, toward the common "works and days" of human life would ever have thought to compose it, or have managed it so cleanly. In the same vein is this single throwaway sentence in the chapter on the *Pequod's* carpenter: "Like all sea-going ship carpenters, and more especially those belonging to whaling vessels, he was, to a certain off-handed, practical extent, alike experienced in numerous trades and callings collateral to his own; the carpenter's pursuit being the ancient and outbranching trunk of all those numerous handicrafts which more or less have to do with wood as an auxiliary material." I cite it here simply for the way in which, in the casual closing phrases, an altogether incidental piece of information has opened out into something larger and curiously moving—into an acknowledgment of that whole humble order of practical arts which lies at the very root of civilization; arts springing from the support given human life by the simplest commodities of nature, and developed in this case by certain aboriginal chippers and carvers from whom we all must acknowledge descent. Though quite unidealizingly, the sentence serves once more to remind us how *Moby-Dick* is not only a melodrama of the catastrophe of one crazed man's overweening defiance and pride, but an unflaggingly heroic celebration of all mankind's laborious tenure of the physical earth.

No account of the setting of *Moby-Dick* in this common world of human labor and effort would be complete without reference to the accompanying conception, periodically renewed and developed with a great variety of illustration, of "man in the ideal"—which is to say, in the large, in history, in legend, in the depths of his natural being, in all the contributing circumstance of his astonishing character and enterprise. In both the inventoried descriptions of whaling and the bouts of violent action, our attention is constantly drawn back to the men of the *Pequod* and those capacities and virtues we are to know them by. During the long middle stretches of the book, Stubb and Queequeg in particular hold the foreground, observed at this or that office of their trade. They are, in a sense, their trade's representative heroes. Yet the coolness under pressure, the flamboyant nonchalance, the unconscious courage and power to learn to associate with them are simply the practical virtues a fortiori of the whole race of seagoing men. (An early précis of these virtues stands out: the high-flown chapter in praise of those "naked Nantucketers" who "live on the sea, as prairie cocks in the prairie," and have marked out two-thirds of the "terraqueous globe" as their empire.) Melville's democratic idealism and glorification of the "kingly commons" are shown as rooted in fact, in the conduct of ordinary men at their ordinary tasks. But as we gradually learn the force and extent of these virtues, we also gradually get a sense of their limits, and an intimation of other and stranger human attributes less readily described though not a bit less real. On the fringes of the main action hover other, weird, unknown races of men —Lascars, Manillas, Parsees—such as "civilized, domesticated people in the temperate zone only see in their dreams, and that but dimly," races full of the "ghostly aboriginalness of earth's primal generations" and testifying to who knows what further depths in the strange creature, man; and these, too, contribute something to the whole context of the developing narrative.

(3) The men of the *Pequod* and their exploits are the practical measure also of the next "world" we can discern in *Moby-Dick*, the non-human world of the sea and the indifferent elements. At the climax of the first lowering after whales, we get a concentrated image of this confrontation of powers, men against nature (it concludes a passage cited by D. H. Lawrence to show Melville's mastery of "violent, chaotic physical motion"). A whale escapes Ishmael's boat; then a squall blows up: "The wind increased to a howl; the waves dashed their bucklers together; the whole squall roared, forked, and crackled

around us like a white fire upon the prairie, in which, unconsumed, we were burning; immortal in the jaws of death." Against the exactly realized violence of the scene, this spectacular assertion of heroism does not seem exorbitant. We note, though, that it is an anonymous, corporate heroism. Man alone, acting individually, comes off less well in this awesome setting, or so chapters like "The Mast-Head" and "The Try-Works" powerfully suggest. A different kind of encounter with the "heartless immensity" of the sea drives the cabin-boy Pip out of his mind, adrift among "strange shapes of the unwarped primal world." And though for Ahab, studying his charts and plotting a course, the sea and its mysteries are (at first) only so many instruments for "the more certain accomplishment of that monomaniac thought of his soul," that seems more and more one further proof of madness in him.

For the great expanse of the sea remains, and dwarfs the most extravagant human pretensions; "two thirds of the fair world it yet covers." Its vastness corresponds ambiguously to the grandeur of Ahab's design—corresponds ironically, of course, insofar as it is literally immeasurable, and wholly indifferent to the character and purposes of men. Its very mildness is tormenting; the haunting descriptions of its moments of sun-burnished serenity, prairie-meadow loveliness, or moonlit quietness are invariably shaded by undertones of another sort, so that the stillness is "preternatural," the beauties are "appalling" and "unearthly," "all space" is felt to be "vacating itself of life," and the mild billows support only such a "formless, chance-like apparition of life" as the giant squid. Prolonged exposure to these weird, uncivil spheres of being, in "exile from Christendom and civilization," reduces men (rather, "restores" them, Melville pointedly writes) to a condition of "savagery." And Ishmael apart, the virtues-in-trade of the men of the *Pequod* are chiefly savage virtues. Their splendor is a primitive splendor that suits their character as great warriors, hunters, migratory navigators, efficient agents all of the hive-disciplined assault on nature; we see that they thrive as creatures in a world of creatures, and that none are better adapted to this world than those ghostly aboriginals (Fedallah is one) from "unchanging Asiatic communities" where the "memory of the first man [is] a distinct recollection."

(4) In the nature of their trade's incessant conflict with the non-human elements, the whalemen are also described as peculiarly subject to superstition and legend-making; the book comes naturally by its solid foothold in folklore. This is not just a consequence of the ignorance, the "savagery," of those sailing before the mast. Starbuck, too, is presented as equally superstitious, though by way of "intelligence" rather than "ignorance," and Ishmael himself is distinguished by a fine readiness of sympathy for everything phantomlike and enigmatical. And it is particularly through Ishmael's thoughtful and excited narrative witness that the free passage of our attention is secured into the final, furthest "world" set out in *Moby-Dick*—the world of "inscrutable" things, unknown depths, unanswerable questions, "ungraspable phantoms," "pyramidical silences," hieroglyphic riddles, "celestial thoughts" which are "to reason absurd and frantic," "bodiless" agents, "sourceless primogenitures" and fatherless specters; a world that communicates to men only in signs, portents, and equivocal omens, and seems intelligible only to madmen like Ahab or Pip, yet is felt at times to control human destinies to the last detail.[5]

Inevitably, in evoking this spectral outer sphere of things, certain words, terms, and concepts are used which, though drawn from commonest usage, may reasonably suggest that

[5] It is this fourth world in particular which is spoken for by the special vocabulary of pluralized participles and noun-abstractions which characterizes Melville's rhetoric at the time of the writing of *Moby-Dick*, just as the book's rich vocabulary of objects and names speaks for the solid environment of "this world." In effect a whole new lexicon of description is created, and it seems to indicate corresponding new doctrines and systems of reality. In *Pierre* this lexicon is entrusted, for long passages, with the whole job of statement, becoming a kind of substitute for concrete observation, and the effect is ruinous—in a weirdly original way.

Melville had some single interpretive scheme for the book as a whole, which it is the job of criticism to identify. Religious allusions are a critical instance of this, and have been a great source of concern to systematizing commentators and exegetes.[6] But when the narrative speaks, in context, of "the interlinked terrors and wonders of God," or relates its heroes' doings to the "mighty, earthly marchings" of the "great democratic God," it does so, I think, without commitment to any identifiable creed or any consistent and paraphrasable "philosophy." Melville's imagination remains, even at these extremities, man-centered and pragmatical. The farthest mysteries of existence remain "those . . . we dream of," and are matched always by the palpable mysteries of human behavior. Consider, for example, the idea of "fate," one of the major terms for the forces conceived to be in play in *Moby-Dick*. By itself, as an independent force, it would be mechanical as a component in the story—and we may well feel that the narrative is least convincing when, in the closing stages, it halfway adopts certain allegoristic conventions of the so-called "fate-tragedy."[7] Only as "fate" is made in one way or another a function of mankind's ordinary and characteristic existence does it take on imaginative validity—when presented, for instance, as a conceit of Ishmael's personal bravado, or, more profoundly, in the haunting evocation of the "weaver-god" (Chapter 102), through the deafening humming of whose ceaseless work the world's "thousand voices" may nevertheless be heard to speak.

[6] On the other hand the standard work on this subject, Nathalia Wright's monograph, *Melville's Use of the Bible* (Durham, 1949), is admirably free of interpretive racking.

[7] The serious claim that an inhuman Fate rules the acts of men comes to us, however, largely through Ahab's late soliloquies and can be understood as a delusion of his monomania. In order to maintain itself, the enormity of pride in him would require the supposition of some worthy supernatural antagonist. Ahab of course is a powerful pleader and will always persuade some readers to see things as he sees them. It is interesting how many interpretations of Melville's masterpieces are written from the point of view of his villains: see the discussion of *Billy Budd* in Chapter Eight, page 198.

So even this final "world" of the unknown and inscrutable is rejoined in *Moby-Dick* to a conception of the life of humankind in time and space. The joining is effected not alone by transcendental correspondences and "linked analogies" (though these are regularly appealed to). The reference is unfailingly to the mortal presence of the species, man. Thus, the thing that is held to be most horror-striking about the sea and its creatures is the knowledge that they preceded man and will survive him. The whale's terrors are "antemosaic" and "unsourced," and they will exist the same "after all human ages are over"; correspondingly, as the book ends, the indifferent sea rolls on again as it did long before men ever went down to it in ships. Still, these "pre-adamite" and post-human ages are not divisible from the span of human history. In passages that tell how the miseries of mortal men descend straight from the aboriginal gods, and how the pre-historic angels "consorted with the daughters of men," Melville appeals in his rough and ready fashion to a myth that a whole succession of hetero-Christian poets and visionaries (consider Blake, Whitman, Yeats, D. H. Lawrence) has found wonderfully seductive—a myth of pre-adamite personages who led a life not unlike ours yet with certain radical exemptions from what we most fear in it: from death, from carnality, from familial combat and dislocation, from the indifferent plenitude of nature, from the blindness of history. Like the conception of fate this myth is ultimately one more way of measuring human experience and feeling. For Melville, it is one means among several of expressing perhaps the furthest intuition in *Moby-Dick*, the intuition of an *anima mundi*, or (to use his words) of a "deep, blue, bottomless soul, pervading mankind and nature," of which the mysterious sea is the prime symbol. All this is most beautifully expressed, I think, in the much remarked chapter in praise of the "mysterious, divine Pacific," as the *Pequod* at last enters its ominous waters—and we may note how the imaginative figure is rendered in terms of the particular souls of individual men:

"There is, one knows not what sweet mystery about this sea, whose gently awful stirrings seem to speak of some hidden soul beneath; like those fabled undulations of the Ephesian sod over the buried Evangelist St. John. And meet it is, that over these sea-pastures, wide-rolling watery prairies and Potters' Fields of all four continents, the waves should rise and fall, and ebb and flow unceasingly; for here, millions of mixed shades and shadows, drowned dreams, somnambulisms, reveries; all that we can lives and souls, lie dreaming, dreaming, still; tossing like slumberers in their beds; the ever-rolling waves but made so by their restlessness."

Set against this image, the career of an Ahab cannot make any finally pre-emptive claim on our concern; and we might well say that in such a passage *Moby-Dick* turns away from the design of tragedy even while dramatically the action is preparing to simulate a tragic denouement. The story of Ahab, we feel, does not quite measure up to its own richest imaginative setting.

A last point. In *Moby-Dick* the various "worlds" which compose the book's setting (and so much of its substance) are not made to cohere philosophically, or allegorically. They need every lodgment in common fact that Melville can manage to give them. They satisfy us as they satisfy our sense of reality. Yet in the descriptive mass of the narrative, subtlety does appeal to subtlety, and Melville, as he builds up and inquires into the contexts that activate his impressive story, and in the process enlarges that very sense of reality, magnificently justifies the challenge he throws out to his reader: that "without imagination no man can follow another into these halls."

CHAPTER FOUR

MELVILLE'S CHARACTERS

> ". . . what is a mortal but a few luckless shovelfuls of clay, moulded into a mould, laid out on a sheet to dry, and ere long quickened into his queer caprices by the sun?"
> —*Israel Potter*, Chapter 23

> ". . . yet the profounder emanations of the human mind, intended to illustrate all that can be humanly known of human life; these never unravel their own intricacies, and have no proper endings; but in imperfect, unanticipated, and disappointing sequels (as multilated things), hurry to abrupt intermergings with the eternal tides of time and fate."—*Pierre*, VII, viii

CRITICS of prose fiction who are concerned with the element of characterization are not likely to offer Melville's narratives as typical evidence. The "novel of character" (if such a thing exists) is not the kind of undertaking we think of him as engaged in. His bent is rather toward forms like the anecdote, the chronicle of related episodes, the "anatomy" (to use Northrop Frye's term)—toward a kind of narrative, that is, in which the individual characters, though perhaps vivid and picturesque enough when directly in view, tend to be subordinate to the general truths or conditions of life which it is the main business of the story to disclose.[1] Yet how roundly, in

[1] If it is true that, in Lawrence Lerner's formula (*The Truest Poetry*, London, 1960, p. 193), "the rise of the novel goes with . . . the concern for people in themselves: not for their symbolic significance, their supernatural backing, their patterning into types, but for their uniqueness," then we may find it hard to think of Melville as a novelist at all. The forms of narrative he works in—the tale of adventure, voyage-description, summary life-history, romance-fable—all have an older provenance than

his best work, Melville's characters occupy the space allotted them; and how easily our imagination opens out to them, how securely they stay in mind. Ahab, Starbuck, Stubb, Queequeg, Pip, Bulkington, Steelkilt, Bildad and Peleg, Father Mapple; Captain Delano and Don Benito Cereno; the Confidence Man, the Missouri bachelor, and indeed the whole motley company or "man-show" of the steamer *Fidèle;* passive Bartleby, stoical Hunilla, Claggart and Vere and Billy Budd; to say nothing of type-characters like Fayaway, Jack Chase, Captain Claret, the Reverend Mr. Falsgrave, Mistress Hussey and Aunt Charity, whose most casual appearance fixes a distinct image: it is an impressive list, and it represents, I think, a major modality of Melville's creative power. Very much the same imaginative freedom and extravagance that we have observed in Melville's settings, and the same truth-abiding search after some vital measure of the common order of earthly existence, direct his rendering of character, and make it equally worth examining, in this inquiry into the actual manner of his performance.

I

Much of what was said in the preceding chapter about the potential interest of descriptions of landscape and setting applies as well to characterization. The image, the composition, will come to life insofar as it is formed out of a generous, thorough, and accurate concern for the real nature and capacity of the human agent; out of an imaginative fidelity, that is, to the observable conditions of his existence. What is perhaps most revealing about Melville's presentation of his characters is his

---

that interest taken by bourgeois society in free-floating individual egos operating within a closed contractual moral scheme, which the form of the nineteenth-century novel classically appeals to. This may help to explain why it is genres such as the saga, the folktale, or the poetic tragedy that seem to provide the best formal parallels for his work.

Of the milieu characteristic of most modern fiction, the film director Vittorio De Sica once remarked: "After all, if you exclude adultery, what drama is there in the bourgeoisie?" See Winthrop Sergeant, "Bread. Love, and Neo-Realismo," *New Yorker,* June 29, 1957.

curiosity about them. Why *are* they what they palpably are? This man is sanguine, that one morose; this one handsome and vital, that one broken and "death-longing"; this one openhearted, that one guarded and cynical; this one literal-minded and wholly practical, that one haunted by doubts and conjectures; this one virtuous and upright (or downright), that one spiritually deformed or "evil"—how in fact have they become so? What circumstance and breeding lie back of them? Through what conditioning have their present features emerged? And what now might they do? What characteristic event is still reserved for them?

For it is not, strictly speaking, in the moral types they exemplify that Melville's characters have their vitality—though most Melville criticism would have us think so—but in the openmindedness, the unremitting inquisitive fascination, of his absorption with them. He is not, at his most effective, a moral fabulist or allegorist but a recorder of life-histories. What his imagination responds to most quickeningly are certain kinds of men ("some men") in whom the conditions of the life of the world ("this world") materialize with beautiful or terrible directness. In this sphere of his performance Melville's address is, as Charles Olson has well defined it, "to character as necessary human force."[2] He is concerned to demonstrate what capacities may be called forth in the creature, man, by the fatalities and accidents of his existence. Like Wordsworth's in *The Prelude,* Melville's sense of life leads him to pursue his concern into "the hiding places of man's power"—not to justify this or that general doctrine of human nature but to bear honest, precise, sympathetic witness to his fascination with the particular display of it. A single sentence of commentary, by the narrator, in a passage of tense, clipped dialogue near the end of the strange tale, "Cock-a-Doodle-Doo!" catches the bare form of this fascination: "The strong soul in the feeble body

[2] "Materials and Weights of Herman Melville," *New Republic,* CXXVIII, September 8 and September 15, 1952.

appalled me." This plain statement, with its contrasted adjectives and strong single verb, resists qualification or rhetorical extension; it effectively gathers up the whole queer force of the story.

And it is in good part because at such moments Melville's inquisitiveness does pass into awe and perplexed wonder that his witness seems peculiarly trustworthy.[3] Several of his characters, particularly in the early books and in those narrative passages that come nearest allegory, do simply embody some abstract moral concept or category of being. But these characters are usually the least satisfactory in themselves; we only tolerate them for the sake of the story, the elsewhere-secured alignment of forces—Fedallah is a fair example. When the character too perfectly represents something foreknown, or something independent of his participation in it, we not only find it hard to believe in him and his behavior, but we may also find it hard to be seriously interested in the idea he is supposed to enforce. One reason why this is so is suggested in one of the several provocative remarks on the principles of fiction scattered about *The Confidence-Man*. Justifying "inconsistent" behavior in one of his characters, Melville appeals to the test of verisimilitude, and asks: "is it not a fact, that, in real life, a consistent character is a *rara avis*?" ". . . if the acutest sage be often at his wit's ends to understand living character, shall those who are not sages expect to run and read character in those mere phantoms which flit along a page, like shadows along a wall? That fiction, where every character can, by reason of its consistency, be comprehended at a glance, either exhibits but sections of character, making them appear for wholes, or else is very untrue to reality. . . ." Melville's sense of the queerness and inconsistency of actual men, including himself ("We are all queer customers, Mr. Duyckinck"), at first richly

[3] Not, however, when it falters too calculatingly and theatrically, as, in *Pierre*, with the characterization of Isabel, who is clumsily pushed out at us, complete with magic guitar, *as* a figure of "mystery."

stimulated, but gradually came to constrict, his effort as a chronicler of human actions. "For whatever is truly wondrous and fearful in man, never yet was put into words or books"—this remark, made late in *Moby-Dick* in reference to the already splendidly realized figure of Queequeg, has the ring of conviction. Coming at that strange moment when, near death, Queequeg's wasted body and lustrous full eyes cause "an awe that cannot be named" to steal over Ishmael, it speaks for Melville's rising obsession with the existence of some impenetrable secret at the roots of every man's life, and for his corresponding insistence on the utter impossibility of real "frankness" on the part of the best-intentioned author. To give up the business of story-telling altogether was only a short step further. For if an inquirer into character comes honestly to believe that the one who best appreciates it is he "who, in view of its inconsistencies, says of human nature the same that . . . is said of the divine nature, that it is past finding out," then his falling silent as before unexaminable mysteries is not surprising. This, I think, is the logical bearing, though it is not the immediate point, of the much-quoted comparison in *The Confidence-Man* of a truly "original" character to a "revolving Drummond light" (Chapter 44), a figure which literally renews the high Romantic association of the writer's imaginative effort with original creation: ". . . everything is lit by it, everything starts up to it . . . so that, in certain minds, there follows upon the adequate conception of such a character, an effect, in its way, akin to that which in Genesis attends upon the beginning of things." After this it would take Melville thirty years to apply himself once more to writing out a complete story; but when at last he did, it was as if he still had this remarkable passage freshly in mind. For in the composed, diffident elevation of its turn of phrase it is in the very style of *Billy Budd*, and the view of the writer's task which it suggests perfectly accords with the extraordinary manner of that story's characterizations of "certain phenomenal men." [4]

[4] See below, Chapter Eight.

II

A different conception of human character from this rapt and indeterminate one is also expressed, and with equal force, all through Melville's books. Presumably, the "originality" in beings whose essential nature is "past finding out" should show itself in conduct which can never be exactly predicted nor reduced to norms and types. Yet elsewhere we find Melville declaring unequivocally that "to treat of human actions is to deal wholly with second causes." This assertion, it is true, was made ten years after *The Confidence-Man*, in the prose "Supplement" to *Battle-Pieces*, where vast impersonal movements of history are being contemplated. But in *Mardi* the philosopher Babbalanja had long before voiced the same unqualified determinism: "Whoso is free from crime, let him cross himself. . . . That he is not bad, is not of him. Potter's clay and wax are all, moulded by hands invisible. The soil decides the man." This is a judgment resumed in *Israel Potter* in the passage quoted at the head of this chapter. In *White-Jacket*, indeed, the whole gallery of characters is sketched according to this general view: that the "ideas" of men are swayed by the "circumstances" of their lives and occupations, and that what they are exposed to in "the jelly of youth" determines their subsequent existence. An entire chapter of *White-Jacket* is cast as a humorous proof of this recurrent thesis: "The Good or Bad Temper of Man-of-War's Men, in a great degree, attributable to their Particular Stations and Duties Aboard Ship." In *The Confidence-Man* the chapter, "Concerning the Metaphysics of Indian-hating," demonstrates the same round truth. And though the stirring elaborations in *Moby-Dick* on the themes of fate and necessity are beyond our concern in this chapter, we may simply observe—to take a single case of some importance to the book as a whole—how in first presenting the character of Starbuck Melville explains the man's qualities in terms of a particular lifelong process of conditioning, and then rounds off his exposition with an explicit statement of what "in reasonable nature" is to be expected of such a man as the story goes forward.

The case of Starbuck suggests the dramatic uses of a deterministic conception of character; it also suggests obvious dramatic limitations. And though Melville often advances this general conception as a sufficient theory of human behavior, it cannot be said to govern his major practice of characterization. Had he been chiefly concerned to demonstrate such a theory for its own sake, as a pre-emptive truth, he might have become a lesser Hardy or a producer at second hand of run-of-the-mill romantic allegory; or perhaps he would have gone the way Mark Twain went in those late, pathetically heartfelt and obsessive fantasies of absolute predestination. What is at the heart of Melville's treatment of his characters, however, is not a philosophy of fate, chance, and free will in the actions of men (though he maneuvers such terms with great freedom and power) but a moral apprehension of the lifelong course of existence natural to the human individual; and it is precisely from the response of the individual actor to the materializing fatality of this course—through his awareness of it as a person, and therefore through his free struggle as a person with the necessities of his history as a creature—that the distinctive Melvillean drama opens out.

Neither the bare assertion of free individuality nor the bare denial of it satisfied Melville's practical sense of the form of men's lives. Their accumulating hostage, his longer narratives demonstrate, is not to any single accident or scheme of fate but to the common sequences of time and change, which are, first, accidental, and, second, irreversible. It is in just this understanding of the common pathos of the careers of men that Melville's characterizations are richest.[5] What each man shares

[5] It is a richness of feeling and imagination rather than of doctrine. From the point of view of philosophy Melville's ideas about character and individual existence are commonplace. But their service in his writing is to the story and the narrative fact—with respect to which they have the high virtues of reasonableness and consistency, as well as a choric suita-

with his kind, in Melville's narrative view, is the plastic capacity to be acted upon and to act in response, a capacity for variation and change within his own life-cycle and the frame of his mortality. In this as in everything else that pertains to individual character, men may differ very greatly. "Yet the difference between this man and that," Melville wrote in *The Confidence-Man,* "is not so great as the difference between what the same man may be to-day, and what he may be in days to come." Against this logic of time and casualty (a Sophoclean logic displaced into Romantic subjectivism) no individual man can hope to prevail, whatever his defenses. "For there is no bent of heart or turn of thought," the same passage continues, "which any man holds by virtue of an unalterable nature and will." This is a "truth" that Melville applies even to an Ahab, whose "unalterable nature and will" are not a bit less the conditioned product of a single course of accident and circumstance than is the pitiful weakness of the most broken and overborne of men. The Melvillean pathos rises most powerfully from the spectacle of these renewed assaults of the "storm of nature" and the "brass" of sheer "events" upon a man's whole habit of thought and sentiment and upon "all his Faith-born, enthusiastic, high-wrought, stoic, and philosophic defenses" (to use the words of a key passage in *Pierre*): "For there is no faith, and no stoicism, and no philosophy, that a mortal man can possibly evoke, which will stand the final test of a real impassioned onset of Life and Passion upon him."

Of course the context and the timing of these dark sayings matter considerably. The melodramatic late stages of *Moby-Dick* and *Pierre,* in particular, are shadowed by Melville's per-

---

bility. They are ideas useful to a chronicler of "actual men and events" (to borrow Melville's phrase for the kind of reading his Captain Vere preferred), and it is as such that they have their real point and force.

But philosophic justification for them is not far to seek. Upon the romantic and transcendentalist celebration of human *nature* and the "infinitude of the private man" (so broadcast in his time as to be second nature to him), Melville may be seen as having interposed a sense of the finite dimension of *history* as a factor in the ordinary life of men.

sonal struggle during 1851 and 1852 with his own inward "storm of nature." We may note even here, though, that the thrust of this rising pessimism is specifically against man's pride in his own thought, against his deliberated moral posture. It is not against man's hold on life; thought and soul may give way, yet something vital will be left, though what it is may be difficult to name. The carpenter in *Moby-Dick* has been reduced to just this extremity, as the narrative meticulously describes him. There is no longer "a common soul" in him, but there remains "a subtle something that somehow anomalously did its duty." He is "remarkable" for "a certain impersonal stolidity . . . that so shaded off into the surrounding infinite of things, that it seemed one with the general stolidity discernible in the whole visible world." Everything personal or circumstantial has in effect been "rubbed off" him. Nevertheless he lives on—"an unfractioned integral," in a "strange uncompromisedness," and "no mere machine of an automaton" either—by virtue of something which Melville calls the "unaccountable, cunning life-principle in him." In the carpenter, it is specified, this life-principle appears to operate mechanically: "his brain, if he ever had one, must have early oozed along the muscles of his fingers." Yet he is as firmly planted on the spectrum of self-operant life shown to us in *Moby-Dick* as any of its figures of valor and power. Moreover, the description of his case curiously complements one of the defining themes of the book: that full-blown celebration of the nobility and grandeur of "man in the ideal" which we find most spectacularly voiced in the first "Knights and Squires" chapter, immediately after the presentation of the admirable Starbuck. For in its indestructible persistence this rooted "life-principle" strangely resembles the element that here is held to be worthiest in mankind: "that immaculate manliness we feel within ourselves, so far within us, that it remains intact though all the outer character seem gone." It is the sense of this element, Ishmael declares, thinking of Starbuck, that makes all men respond "with keenest anguish" to a noble hero's undoing. So the carpenter's sad history, in being thus reduced, is but a primitive form of that shocking "fall of valor in the soul" which, to Ishmael, will be the "thing most sorrowful" in all that he has to tell.

A man's thought and character, even his soul, may thus fail, in the Melvillean scheme, being only products of circumstance, yet some vital essence remain untouched. And alongside the circumstantial or determinist explanation of character in Melville's writing runs this counter-theme of the irreducibility of the force of life in the human creature. *White-Jacket* especially, with its "free, broad, man-of-war" outlook, develops this emphasis. We hear of the "untouchableness of true dignity" that can bring men safely through the degradation of a flogging; or of that feeling of "bottomless manhood" which gives the sailor Nord his profound fear of unjust punishment, and old Ushant his power to endure it. Deeper yet, we are reminded of the simplest instinct of life that is in every earthly creature, an instinct "diffused through all animate nature, the same that prompts even a worm to turn under the heel." It is this instinct that drives White Jacket himself, under threat of the scourge, to the frantic project of mutinous murder.[6] This last example is somewhat equivocal, I grant, for his action, White Jacket admits, would also have been suicide; and it thus would have violated the plainest declaration of creed that Melville ever offered, the declaration in *Mardi* (Chapter xiii) that "the only true infidelity is for a live man to vote himself dead." What Melville seems to have prized with least qualification in human character is the free manifestation of this primordial instinct of life—as in his celebration in *White-Jacket* of the "infantile, sinless look" which shines out of the eye of a certain patriarchal mainmast-man, and which is "the same that answered the glance of this old man's mother when first she

[6] See *Pierre*, xxv, ii, on that "pride-horror," at the possibility of public disgrace, which is, to "a proud and honorable man," "more terrible than any fear."

cried for the babe to be laid by her side." The force of instinct in that look is nothing less than man's warrant for eternity, for it expresses, Melville concludes, "the fadeless, ever infantile immortality within."

The philosophic cogency of these last passages, the practical value of their apparent identification of virtue with something "infantile" and "sinless," I leave for the moment to the consideration of those dealers in speculative currencies who would make Melville's "ideas" the great measure of his importance. The perfection of such ideas in formal expression is what immediately concerns us in assessing his example as a writer. His apprehension of his characters is not subsumed in his aphorisms about them. These supply at best the moral co-ordinates of the particular station of being each one has come to occupy. The moral nature of the personae of Melville's fiction cannot be summed up except in terms of the material situations and actions he shows them engaged in. And the significant differences among them, or between one stage and another of their recorded lives, are differences in the manner, the vital posture, of this active engagement. Perhaps the most original division of character Melville's work offers, and the one, I think, that throws the most piercing light on his moral imagination, is that between the "compromised" and the "uncompromised"—between those who are wholly subdued as persons to the conditions of their existence, and those few others who, though having no greater power to overcome these conditions, nevertheless maintain identity, or keep countenance, within them.[7]

[7] The one type of being for whom Melville shows least sympathy is the man who has held himself back from either of these potentially tragic states, the man compromised not by life but by the negatives of self-interest. This is what the Ishmael-like Missouri bachelor scornfully labels "the moderate man." With his "picked and prudent sentiments," the Missouri bachelor sneers, this "moderate man" is simply "the invaluable understrapper of the wicked man." "You, the moderate man, may be used for wrong, but are useless for right." (*The Confidence-Man*, Chapter 21).

For an out-and-out villain like Claggart in *Billy Budd*, on the other hand, Melville shows a profound inquisitive compassion.

There are common, worldly forms of this latter condition, and some of Melville's most effective characterizations participate in it—good-humored Stubb, for example, with his "invulnerable jollity," or the flamboyant case of "coolness" embodied in Queequeg; and we recognize such characterizations as representative of Melville's happiest vein of comedy. The "strange uncompromisedness" of the carpenter marks him as another such, though by virtue only of "a kind of deaf and dumb, spontaneous literal process" which is "half-horrible" to contemplate. The same language of identification is used for the more significant case of "tender-hearted" Pip, who, in being cast away, passes from cowardice into a light-headed insanity indistinguishable from "celestial" wisdom—in which transformed state, the narrative specifies, a man will feel himself "uncompromised, indifferent as his God." Of all the company of the *Pequod,* Pip alone touches Ahab's "humanity" to the quick. And the charged language of this episode of Pip's transformation into an impotent but clairvoyant madness may recall an earlier passage in *Moby-Dick* in which, for once, Ahab's full measure as a moral being is taken; this is the tantalizing reference in Chapter 33 to a certain transcendent order of persons ("God's true princes") defined only as "the choice hidden handful of the Divine Inert," with respect to whom even such a hero as Ahab must seem of an "infinite inferiority."

Except perhaps for Pip, this mysterious breed is absent from the mechanical fate-tragedy that *Moby-Dick* almost resolves into. But something of what Melville may have meant by the category of the "Divine Inert" appears plainly enough in his work of 1853–1856. Among the stories written during these already overshadowed years we find a series of characters who are identified, and made exemplary, by their strange power of passive endurance of their life's life-destroying conditions. There is the "stranger," mute, fair-haired, "lamb-like," whose coming aboard the steamboat *Fidèle* opens *The Confidence-Man.* There is the Chola widow of the eighth "Encantadas" sketch, in whom we are asked to observe "nature's pride subduing nature's torture." And there is pale, mild Bartleby, with his irresistible fidelity to his negative "preferences." That these last two, Hunilla and Bartleby, came to represent for Melville some general truth about the capacity and fortune of the human creature is made clear by the choric invocation which the story of each pointedly rises to.[8] Their impressiveness was not lost on Melville's best readers in 1853 and 1854. Given the failure with his public of Ahab and Pierre, his most ambitious characterizations, one notices now with special pleasure the elder R. H. Dana's pronouncement to Evert Duyckinck that the story of Bartleby "touches the nicer strings of our complicated nature," and James Russell Lowell's comment in a letter to Melville's editor at Putnam's that he thought the ending of the tale of Hunilla "the finest touch of genius he had seen in prose."

III

As the event goes, or has gone, the man comes into his identity, an identity which will then prove more or less capable (by an economy that in each case may be named but perhaps never wholly understood) of maintaining itself within its acquired course of life. Such seems to be Melville's sense of the formation of human character. We rarely, however, see this formation taking place in his stories. The tale of moral or psychological growth is one of the major productive conventions of nine-

[8] In "Bartleby," by the closing words: "Ah, Bartleby! Ah, humanity!" In "The Encantadas" sketch, by the phrase climaxing the narrator's extended intrusion in his own voice midway in his story: "Humanity, thou strong thing. . . ."

Another character cut to this general pattern, though not made so broadly emblematic, is John Marr (*Collected Poems*, pp. 159–166), an old man holding on to life in desolation and solitude by virtue of the unfading phantoms of memory. The half-dozen unassertive pages of prose prefacing his verse-soliloquy make up a perfect instance of Melville's manner of characterization: the circumstantial skein of a life-history leading to one or two defining moments and their precisely revealing gestures. From the sketch of John Marr one could draw out, I think, very nearly the whole conception of "character" which has been traced so far in this chapter.

teenth-century fiction; but when Melville undertakes it directly, as in *Mardi* and *Pierre,* he appears, formally, at his weakest. *Redburn* begins as though in this mode, but does not keep to it once the "first voyage" is underway. In *Moby-Dick* Ahab's madness has overtaken him before the *Pequod* sails, while Ishmael fixes his own persona with his famous first breath; in fact, most of the characters are categorically defined for us before they lift a finger in action. The method of characterization is explanatory and descriptive rather than dramatic.

Yet I think it may be shown that Melville's characterizations, as much as any other factor, are what give dramatic life and movement to the structure of his best writing. A successful piece of narrative fiction is a progression of formal events which are persuasive both in their general logic and sequence and also in their constituent parts. The arrangement of the whole must hold together, so as positively to accomplish its large effects; but it will not do so unless there is life and truth in the words and things of each successive part, and a steady return of immediate satisfaction. Style alone is not enough, nor is a system of interlocking analogies, however efficiently worked out. The composition will need some rough, plain, natural shorthand of demonstration and reference which will be quickly intelligible to the reader, and of course sufficiently entertaining in its own part, and which will save the writer from having to establish *ab novo* the interest and bearing of each new unit of narration.

In the central mass of *Moby-Dick*—to take the most impressive single case of Melville's compositional skill—the characterizations, and in particular the figures of Stubb and Queequeg, perform a very great part of this tactical service. How, we may ask, would *Moby-Dick* manage without this sturdy pair? Studying the book as a table of ethical types and values, as W. H. Auden has done in *The Enchaféd Flood*, we may see them as subordinate integers at best. So for Auden, Stubb, defined as the man "unable to face suffering," is neither more nor less important than the other mates, who stand for other forms of spiritual cowardice, while Queequeg, held to represent the "unconscious pagan world" of natural appetite, is rather less significant than, say, Pip or Fedallah.[9] But simply following the narrative along, chapter by chapter, we may come to a different rating of their importance. For more than two hundred pages in the middle of *Moby-Dick*, between the first lowering and the ship's climactic emergence into the Pacific, Stubb and Queequeg are, in frequency of appearance, very nearly its principal actors. In that part of the book which is a meditative-heroic poem on the honor and glory, and practical enterprise, of whaling, they are (the narrator apart) the figures of first prominence among the *Pequod's* company, and they are instruments of the first importance in securing the impression of reality on the grand scale of Melville's conceiving.

It would be easy to exaggerate this point. *Someone*, presumably, must be on hand to perform the labors which are to be tabulated and described. Also, the prominence of Stubb and Queequeg is a relative thing; for every passage in which they are called forth in aid of the exposition, there are two or three others in which the narrator's meditative fancy works alone. But it is precisely in counterpointing this first-person discourse, and underscoring its probings with the natural emphasis of their special prowess, that they repeatedly give pace and vitality to the progress of the narrative—a function for which the quality of character Melville has troubled to establish in them pre-

[9] In effect, however, this is to judge the events of the book from Ahab's demented point of view—as Melville did not, except when he edged over into mechanical allegory in certain late chapters. To Ahab, Stubb is nothing more than an especially convenient target for his scornful opinion of the ordinary race of "manufactured" men, whom he is compelled to rely on; and Queequeg, too, is of interest to him only as a fine "tool"—or, in the hieroglyphic mysteries of his tattooing, as an equally impersonal "tantalization of the gods."

Auden's comments on Stubb simply ignore the rough vitality and charm of the second mate's nature, and—this is more to the point—Melville's obvious pleasure in it.

cisely fits them. Of Stubb especially is this true. No more consequential example can be cited—since it is the success of *Moby-Dick* that is at stake—of Melville's way of projecting a character by means of a few explanatory epithets and designations, and then allowing him the freedom of action to convince us of the reality both of his own being and of all that the narrative shows him engaged in.

Stubb's moral type is quickly established. He is "calm," "cool," "off-handed," "indifferent" to danger or the thought of death, a "high liver" attentive to his own rugged comforts, and above all "humorous." From the first we know his ultimate limits of spirit, the something mechanical about his fearlessness, the "almost impious" quality of his good humor. For describing the everyday business of whaling, however, he is the man Melville needs. More than once Stubb's boat is "foremost" in pursuit of the whale; it is he who is most often seen in the chase and at the kill, and who also has the laborious office of overseeing the work of boiling down. He perfectly exemplifies the workaday, democratic skillfulness, on a heroic scale where "dignity and danger go hand in hand," that Melville proposes to celebrate. So we are asked to marvel at Stubb's deftness in decapitating the huge, thick-fleshed, neckless sperm whale, half under a rolling sea, in ten minutes' time; and we are commanded to take special note of his excellence in the fine art of pitchpoling. He exemplifies no less flamboyantly the commercial motive at the heart of the whole business of whaling, as by "unrighteous cunning" (though also by superior knowledge of the details of his trade) he tricks a French whaler out of a cache of ambergris. He is continually presented to us as an ingenious, inventive, devising man, cheerfully at home among the violent necessities of his work.

Now by abstracting this character from the uses Melville puts it to, it is possible to draw up a severe moral indictment of it—as Auden does in stressing Stubb's declared indifference to whatever passes his practical understanding. In the matter of abandoning Pip on the empty ocean, Stubb, according to Auden, is "guilty of destroying an innocent boy's sanity": "He does not guess what the consequences of leaving Pip in the water will be, because he has never really looked at him." To which it can only be answered that though the indictment may well apply, Melville himself does not think to press it. Stubb has already saved Pip's life once, breaking off the chase to do it, and is only speaking the world's plain truth in reminding the slave-boy that one whale is worth thirty Pips on the open market. At another point we see Stubb bedeviling the old negro cook (a figure of fun, be it said, out of the crudest popular tradition); but we also see him forcefully interceding for Queequeg in behalf of his right to a proper ration of grog. The point is that he knows the value of every tool and every man in his hazardous service, and acts accordingly, with impressive dispatch. The cook's remark that Stubb is "more of shark dan Massa Shark hisself" is a just and, in the circumstances of the book, an honorific tribute.

Queequeg does not appear as often as Stubb in these middle chapters of *Moby-Dick*, but plays, in his own even cooler and calmer pagan manner, the same kind of role. He is a comparably heraldic figure in the celebration of the arts and mysteries of whaling. (In these passages we are only incidentally reminded of his relationship to Ishmael in the New Bedford chapters.) He, too, is singled out in the narrative to perform various tasks of professional skill: drawing the whale's teeth, delivering Tashtego out of the well of sperm in its huge head, fencing off sharks from its floating corpse, riding its slippery back to drive in the blubber-hook, managing the delicate and exhausting business of stowing the oil casks in the hold, and so on. To these competences the savage Queequeg adds, naturally enough, some that are all his own. He has a special alertness to physical signs and omens; he it is, for example, who happens to remember that where squid have been seen, sperm whales may be expected. Everything he does is on a prodigious scale, as befits the setting and action of the story, yet is performed with the "indifferent promptitude" of his savage nature. He is a magnificent creature in a world of magnificent creatures, mutually sympathetic. Thus the cannibalism he was bred to corresponds to the "universal cannibalism" of the sea, whose most savage monsters have no spiritual terror for him. But in this, too, civilized Stubb matches him, for it is Stubb's epicurean meal of whale-steak, and his thus devouring "a newly murdered thing of the sea, and . . . by his own light," that leads the narrator to exclaim concerning carnivorous mankind: "Cannibals? who is not a cannibal?"

A sense of Stubb's fitness, in particular, for pointing up certain main themes and emphases seems to have grown on Melville as he worked along, for Stubb's prominence in the narrative does not diminish in the Ahab-dominated climax of it. He makes as good a commentator on certain dramatic incidents as Ishmael, and Melville uses him fitfully all through the last hundred pages as a point of reference for the main action. Stubb's "humorousness" matches one major mood of Ishmael's witness, and provides the same kind of contrasts. In his own habitual style he takes Fedallah's measure, we notice, from the start, and more than once siphons off our own dangerous sense of Fedallah's ludicrousness as a symbolic agent.[10] He takes Ahab's measure, too; the carpenter insists, in fact, that Stubb is the one who knows Ahab "best of all." The narrator of course "knows" more; yet it may be pointed out that Stubb's quick response to Ahab's display of concentrated pride and purpose—"damn me, Ahab, but thou actest right; live in the game, and die in it!"—speaks as centrally for Melville's multiple apprehension of his hero's nature as does, say, Father Mapple's glorification of "him . . . who against the proud gods and commodores of this earth, ever stands forth his own inexorable

[10] See Chapter 99, "The Doubloon": " 'But, aside again! here comes that ghost-devil, Fedallah; tail coiled out of sight as usual, oakum in the toes of his pumps as usual.' "

self." To the end Stubb's impulsive sympathy for Ahab holds strong, and his rising excitement as the catastrophe comes on is dramatic vindication of Ahab's conduct—though the mad captain still scorns him.[11]

An especially interesting case of Stubb's accumulating usefulness as a character is his part in the chapter called "The Doubloon." Two pages along in this masque-like survey of ways of interpreting the world's emblematic mysteries, he steps forward and takes over as impresario and chorus (mad Pip, of course, is given the last word). In such appearances Stubb comes very near representing the narrative point of view, or one main element in it. In his own proper character he perfectly embodies that "free and easy sort of genial, desperado philosophy" especially bred by whaling, Ishmael tells us, but also natural to all the "queer times and occasions in this strange mixed affair we call life when a man takes this whole universe for a vast practical joke. . . ." ". . . nothing dispirits, and nothing seems worth disputing. He bolts down all events, all creeds, and beliefs, and persuasions, all hard things visible and invisible, never mind how knobby; as an ostrich of potent digestion gobbles down bullets and gun flints." "Queer" is Stubb's "one sufficient little word" for all the mysteries he encounters; and it is a perfectly accurate word as far as it goes, though schoolmaster Ishmael can always think of a few more.

IV

The two attempts at full-scale dramatic characterization in Melville's work are Ahab and Pierre. It may seem unnecessary to remark that the first is on the whole the more effective. Yet if anything comes near to spoiling *Moby-Dick* it is the presentation of Ahab as a personal agent in the drama; and if anything comes near to saving *Pierre* it is the presentation of the un-

[11] It would be less than fair to Stubb not to point out that he makes the best end of the three mates. So it seems to me, at least; Auden, however, considers his last words evasive and childish.

folding inward nature, capable of passional action and change, of its otherwise preposterous hero (who is hardly more preposterous, however, than the type of the free-born young male, on the edge of manhood, in actual life). The characterization of Ahab can succeed because *Moby-Dick* as a whole does not depend on it. Its strength is borrowed from the strength of the whole recital of which it is a part (including the brazenly suspenseful plot of the hunt after a fabulous creature). Its chief artistic virtue is its consistency with what is elsewhere revealed, defined, and rehearsed in this extraordinary book. The characterization of the young Pierre, on the other hand, is in certain ways a more thoughtful and potentially a more interesting undertaking; but there is little else in the book capable of supporting it, or of bringing the crude formal conventions it is encased by back into living reality.

In *Moby-Dick* the essential character of Ahab is established in a rather curious way—well before he puts in an appearance, almost before he is even named. This is done in the much-quoted passage in Chapter 16, "The Ship," which describes the general breed of Nantucket whale-hunter. Here the figure is sketched of a man of "audacious, daring, and boundless adventure," possessing "a globular brain and a ponderous heart," who has been led by his course of life to think "untraditionally and independently," and who now stands forth as "a mighty pageant creature, formed for noble tragedies," but who also exhibits a certain "half wilful over-ruling morbidness at the bottom of his nature." With the addition of two or three further generalizations, a few pages later, by Captain Peleg, the characterization of Ahab is now virtually complete. Successive chapters—describing his appearance on the quarterdeck, the vision of him in Stubb's dream, and his sultanic overlordship on the *Pequod*—amplify it, but mostly by the same kind of type-defining, the same application of descriptive labels and epithets. It is as though some vast and changeless phenomenon of physical nature was being analyzed and explained, according to the logic of its prehistoric formation (so that there is a fine appropriateness to the borrowing of Hotspur's rhetoric that closes out Chapter 33: "Oh, Ahab! what shall be grand in thee, it must needs be plucked at from the skies, and dived for in the deep, and featured in the unbodied air!"). Ahab's first long speeches, in Chapters 36 and 37, have the same essentially explanatory function—though we notice that in their overwrought style and floundering organization they are distinctly less effective, even dramatically, than the strong, well-paced analytic writing in those chapters immediately succeeding (Chapters 41, 44, 46), to which the main exposition of Ahab's case is entrusted.

Mad from the beginning, Ahab makes a strange and awesome figure but not, in the main, one arousing tragic pity and fear. The sublimity of his posture and the astonishing energy of his "monomania" are skillfully indicated. But perhaps the most impressive single paragraph about him is one (Chapter 41) in which the direct rendering of his individual being is abandoned altogether, and the job of suggesting the real presence in him of some "larger, darker, deeper part," that contains his "State-secret" and "whole awful essence," is assigned to an elaborate descriptive metaphor of the spiked Hôtel de Cluny in Paris and the weird, timeless Roman ruins beneath it. The role Ahab is given to play is an earnest of Melville's drive and ambition in the book. But the characterization itself is static in conception, and contrived and mechanical in the actual working out. Ahab acts most of the time in a trance of calculating madness; or, to put it in another way, he stays monotonously within the mold established for him.[12] The vitality and persuasiveness of the narrative are chiefly secured, I have already suggested, by other means. Yet there are moments of genuine poignancy in the presentation of Ahab that enrich the whole book, most

[12] "Thus a man lasts but a very little while, for his monomania becomes insupportably tedious in a few months." (Emerson, "The Method of Nature.")

notably the touching interlude of Chapter 132, "The Symphony," in which for once he steps briefly out of his appointed role and questions it, in Starbuck's presence, from his "own proper, natural heart." Also, in the final chapters, the theatrical contrivance of this role does emerge as thoroughly in keeping with the splendidly theatrical effectiveness of the long three-act climax.

With Ahab Melville projected, and brought off, a great effect; with the hero of *Pierre* he aimed at nothing less than the "sacred truth." The imaginative strength of this disordered book is in its oddly angled but deeply measured insight into the common pathos of human becoming; and as it pursues this excellent subject, as it tries to define the developing action of the human soul's natural history, I think it moves rather closer to the specific dimension of tragedy than does *Moby-Dick.*[13] It falls very short, of course—but only by a technical incompetence so extraordinary as to be of no real technical interest. The characterization of Pierre is subordinated (as it should be) to the shifting display of passion and motive within him, a display that registers more impressively than would seem possible, given the preposterousness of the story. Where this characterization is most effective, it is as largely explanatory and descriptive, rather than dramatic, as that of Ahab. And it is even more impersonal. All the particular detail that encumbers it—the Gorgon's faces, chair portraits, Semiramian mothers, enchantress half-sisters, and sacrificial sweethearts, the primeval pine trees, Memnon stones, dreams of Enceladus, Flaxman's Dantes, Plinlimmon's pamphlets, Hamletries and Timonisms—seems no more, with respect to the hero's real history, than those "mere contingent things" marking the "endless, winding way,—the flowing river in the cave of man," which Melville pledges himself to trace out. They matter only as they relate to the empirical phenome-

[13] So Yeats might have thought: "Tragedy is passion alone, and rejecting character, it gets form from motives, from the wandering of passion. . . ." ("Estrangement: Extracts from a Diary Kept in 1909," section xxiv.)

non of the natural progress of the soul, or growth of the mind, which is the book's true subject.

Various kinds of sentence intended to define what is happening within Pierre may be cited to indicate the shifts and changes in this peculiar scheme of characterization. The effort to present Pierre's condition directly, or dramatically, tends to produce passages like the following, which is justly notorious: "Now indeed did all the fiery floods in the Inferno, and all the rolling gloom in Hamlet suffocate him at once in flame and smoke. The cheeks of his soul collapsed in him: he dashed himself in blind fury and swift madness against the wall, and fell dabbling in the vomit of his loathed identity." Rather less grotesque is the attempt, at one remove from direct action, to record Pierre's own sense of his developing condition: "He felt that what he had always before considered the solid land of veritable reality, was now being audaciously encroached upon by bannered armies of hooded phantoms, disembarking in his soul, as from flotillas of specter-boats." This is still too much in the vein of the specter-allegories of *Mardi*, but at least the metaphor has a certain crude definiteness of outline, and is attached to an intelligible moment of feeling. Better yet, and better in proportion to the greater rational coherence and independent force of the analogy, is the following sentence concerning a later moment in Pierre's progress: "Now he sees that with every accession of the personal divine to him, some great landslide of the general surrounding divineness slips from him, and falls crashing away." This is equally orotund, perhaps; yet its cadences effectively emphasize the active form of what it has to say. And what it has to say is rather grandly impressive. At least we may note that the sentence turns cleanly upon the two poles of one of the vital preoccupations of Romantic and transcendentalist thinking, the correspondence of the individual soul and the animating spirit of the universe. This introduction of philosophic analogy into the narrative is indeed a potential virtue in the book. The very impressionableness and malleability of the youthful Pierre make it wholly reasonable for each stage in his characterization to take the overform of a critique of thoughts and ideas, or, we might say, to serve as the kind of "rendezvous of problems" Gide intended in constructing his *Faux-Monnayeurs* around a group of schoolboys.

But it is when Melville's concern is not with the substance of Pierre's thought but with the mysterious process of his arriving at it and being acted upon by it that the writing most successfully rescues itself from bombast and from emblem-mongering. At such moments the narrative is likely to back off from the plot, and view altogether impersonally, and analytically, its announced subject, that "maturer and larger interior development" promised in Pierre. Certainly that is what is happening in this remarkable paragraph-long sentence:

"If it be the sacred province and—by the wisest, deemed—the inestimable compensation of the heavier woes, that they both purge the soul of gay-hearted errors and replenish it with a saddened truth; that holy office is not so much accomplished by any covertly inductive reasoning process, whose original motive is received from the particular affliction; as it is the magical effect of the admission into man's inmost spirit of a before unexperienced and wholly inexplicable element, which like electricity suddenly received into any sultry atmosphere of the dark, in all directions splits itself into nimble lances of purifying light; which at one and the same instant discharge all the air of sluggishness and inform it with an illuminating property; so that objects which before, in the uncertainty of the dark, assumed shadowy and romantic outlines, now are lighted up in their substantial realities; so that in these flashing revelations of grief's wonderful fire, we see all things as they are; and though, when the electric element is gone, the shadows once more descend, and the false outlines of objects again return; yet not with their former power to deceive; for now, even in the presence of the falsest aspects, we still retain the impressions of their immovable true ones, though, indeed, once more concealed."

Here, while it is a moral sense of the mind's character-fixing sequences of feeling and awareness that animates the passage, it is an objective inquisitiveness about their actual mechanism of operation that sustains the detailed figure and bodies forth the argument. Melville is most likely to write well in *Pierre* when he is most analytic. The discipline of exact description is, once again, what gives form and point to the rhapsodical "swearing" he confessed to Hawthorne that he was prone to "in the last stages of metaphysics." There is little use in trying to imagine how the book as a whole might have been salvaged. It is enough to say that the protracted characterization *Pierre* is mainly built upon is, potentially, as compatible with the illimitable art of prose fiction as are the analytic meditations of a Proust—whose practice of character-description the long sentence just quoted may well call to mind. Both Melville and Proust were concerned to anatomize the behavior of individual human persons in the light of certain profounder necessities of human nature; and both grounded their inquiries in more or less systematic conceptions of what, morally, their findings must finally amount to. Of course this method of characterization will be most successful when the analysis and exposition are firmly in the service of some serious and absorbing *story*, such as in their major work both these writers did have to tell.

CHAPTER FIVE

MELVILLE'S NARRATORS

"If to affirm, be to expand one's isolated self; and if to deny, be to contract one's isolated self; then to respond is a suspension of all isolation."—*Pierre*, XXI, iii

IT WILL have been noticed in the preceding chapter that nothing was said about one main class of Melville's characters, those narrators in the first person who in all his earlier books more or less steadily hold the center of the stage. But the omission was not arbitrary, for these figures form a class apart in his fiction. They are, of course, imaginative creations, not less than his other characters. Though Melville is writing as if autobiographically, the persona of the narrator is never the same as the author's but is projected in each case according to the scheme of presentation, and the tone, adopted for the book as a whole. And in each case, intermittently, this persona is made to play its part with as artificial an absorption and single-mindedness (or "unreserve," to use one of Melville's words) as any hero of conventional melodrama.

Nevertheless the obvious fact is that Melville's work stands, in the main, well apart from what were becoming the major conventions of the nineteenth-century novel, and his use of first-person narration is a leading aspect of its irregularity. The types of fiction he most often chose to start from were not the dramatic or the "well-made" novel, nor the novel of character or of manners, nor even the "romance," but the personal adventure-chronicle, the recital, the confession, in all of which the interposing of a narrator's voice tends to become the chief formal precipitant of interest and of significance. The case is the same with his best later work. "Bartleby the Scrivener," "I and My Chimney," in fact all his magazine pieces between 1853 and 1856 except "Benito Cereno" and "The Bell-Tower," are told in the first person; while in longer efforts like *Israel Potter, The Confidence-Man,* and, years later, *Billy Budd,* the author speaking in his own voice enters freely into the telling of the story, and opportunities for objective representation and dramatic climax seem almost obstinately disregarded.

It needs to be said at once that this method of narration is not necessarily a poor substitute for a higher art of fiction which Melville could not master. The method of the first-person recital or chronicle exists in its own right, with its own reserve of enabling conventions. It is not, for one thing, bound to that ideal of a fabricated unity of dramatic demonstration, transmitted through a correspondingly unbroken illusion of dramatic immediacy, which some theorists of the novel have seemed to put forward as the form of forms into which the arts of prose fiction have been biologically evolving. Its kinship is instead with certain older types of narrative, usually in good part documentary—voyage and travel relations, confessional recitals, descriptive or peregrinative forms of satire and allegory—in all of which we find a broadly consistent moral point of view directly and confidentially expressed and carried episodically through a panorama of picturesque occasions and events. The value of the work will be in the power and scope of this point of view, and in the imaginative coherence, dramatic or otherwise, of the successive episodes.

It is worth remarking that these irregular types of narrative, in or out of the first-person voice, have come strongly back into high favor in twentieth-century writing, and underlie some of its most notable innovations; their revival indicates a serious dissatisfaction with the well-made, dramatic norm. At the same time we may take particular note of the very widespread use of first-person narrative, for some writers almost prescriptive, in American letters: from Brockden Brown's novels and many of Poe's tales, through *The Blithedale Romance, Huckleberry Finn, The Country of the Pointed Firs, The Great Gatsby, The Sun Also Rises, I Thought of Daisy, The Sound and the Fury,* and *Tropic of Cancer,* down to the more interesting work since 1945—*All the King's Men, The Catcher in the Rye, Augie March* and *Henderson the Rain King, The Untidy Pilgrim, Love Among the Cannibals*—to say nothing of such, literally, inimitable books as *Walden, Leaves of Grass,* and *The Enormous Room.* (The exceptions are chiefly among the novels of the "realist" and "naturalist" writers, in the period of Howells, James, Norris, and Dreiser, with their special deference to nineteenth-century European models and to, in some degree, a documentary, sociological, or scientific conception of truth.) Thus, to examine Melville's use of this interesting method is apparently to touch upon formal properties common to a main American tradition of imaginative writing. It may also be to touch upon the social logic underlying that tradition—though what little I have to say in this respect is mostly reserved for the next chapter; here my concern is simply with the tactics of the first-person method, and with its returns.

Its basic virtue, just as with the more artfully designed Jamesian novel, is veracity or the "air of reality." And the indispensable practical requirement it must satisfy is simply to be interesting. Without an ability to rouse the reader's attention and confidence—an ability that does seem, with those who possess it, one of the more natural or spontaneous of the expressive arts—the game of persuasion can be lost at the outset. Given this ability, the first-person method at once shows certain positive advantages. It allows for (though it does not automatically justify) an exploratory looseness and variety in organization and an easy freedom of inclusion; the binding and verifying personal presence of the speaker gives margin, and opportunity, for that casual digressiveness which in support of a strong theme can help to secure the illusion of natural life and truth. With respect to the materials for fiction this method can open up certain enlivening new resources, those for example of folktale and popular anecdote. To style it can help to restore mimetic freshness, and colloquial muscle. To the flow of narrative it can give the quick urgency of personal testimony, the insinuating authority of the truly sincere. Its advantage above all is in gaining direct access to those "effects of actuality and intimacy" which Robert Frost once impulsively spoke up for as "the greatest aim an artist can have." [1]

There are also evident disadvantages—narrowness of range once the sustaining voice is secured, shortness of staying power, monotony of accent and effect. The point of view need not be strictly realistic and can take on, more easily than with the dramatized novel, the special power of implication of fantasy, fable, or legend; but not less than in more tightly constructed fiction the point of view must remain consistent with the possible stuff of the story, and must continue receptive and flexible before all the story's local pressures toward expansion and crystallization. In fact the more decisively the opening passages focus attention, the more difficult it may be to vary the angle and broaden the scope later on. That is why the first-person method seems to lend itself best to shorter forms—the tale, the anecdote, the sketch, the narrative essay. There, these effects of actuality and intimacy may be concentrated within a single compact set of circumstances. Also, such considerations may help to explain why in writing *Redburn* Melville, having begun his hero's "sailor-boy confessions" with a more restrictively naturalistic characterization than was usual with him, was obliged to change his tactics and voice a third of the way through the book, as his purposes expanded.

Of the tonal effects of first-person adventure-narrative Poe was the original American master. But he could bring them off only in the kind of single-minded composition he defined in

[1] Letter to W. S. B. Braithwaite, March 22, 1915, quoted in Elizabeth Shepley Sergeant, *Robert Frost: The Trial by Existence* (New York, 1960), pp. 163–164.

his famous review of Hawthorne's tales. If one characteristic opening sentence of Poe's, "Let me call myself, for the present, William Wilson," with its neat appeal to the reader's connivance, typifies the spectacular economy by which his best tales drive to their single impressions, another first sentence, the flat "My name is Arthur Gordon Pym" that launches his one novel-length effort, may recall his corresponding lack of interest in more complex forms. Both sentences, in any case, point up the wonderful resonance of *Moby-Dick's* famous "Call me Ishmael." Melville's bluff appropriation of a mythical identity indicates a more commanding moral outlook than we are likely to find in Poe's tales; yet in its severe grammatical simplicity it does not restrict itself to any one avenue of development, but keeps all possibilities open.

All these first sentences, we observe, have one function in common. They do not really identify the character or condition of the speaker, though they give clear hints.[2] But they do begin the action of establishing the direct contact with the reader, the mutual confidence, the communion even, that the first-person method of narration is built upon. The whole recital becomes a prolonged conspiracy between "I" and "you." The burden of maintaining it is of course on the speaking "I," but it turns out to be an easy one to carry, at least on a modest scale. Only a radical or protracted violation of the ordinary willing reader's grant of confidence will discourage him entirely. For the reader has as much at stake in the success of their conspiracy as the writer. "I could inform the dullest author how he might write an interesting book," Coleridge told Thomas Poole. "Let him relate the events of his own life with honesty, not disguising the feelings that accompanied them." If by the persuasiveness of his testimony the first-person narrator does

[2] It might be said of Melville that there are many proper "Ishmaels" in his books, but that the narrator of *Moby-Dick* is not necessarily one of them. There is indirection in these first words; there may be irony. "Call me Ishmael—and see whether, and in what way, I am the man you took me for."

confirm the reality of his own being and presence, the reader's assent proves, pro tempore, the reality of *his;* both come to life, for the duration of the telling, by their shared engagement in a thus personally-vouched-for order of existence. The form that results bears the mark of this collaboration and answers to its logic. It builds, that is, on an agreement to accept the encountered world of common experience as the real world of men's existence; this is true of course even when it is put to the special uses of satire and mockery. That is why the mode of first-person narrative is essentially a comic mode, in the broadest sense. For the great theme of the comic, in Northrop Frye's words, is precisely "the integration of society"; it presumes, that is, the acceptability, the viability for civil ends, of that fundamental social contract (based on an assumption of the stability of the real world) which it is the initial effect of tragic experience to subvert and deny and which only the more intense and hieratic art of tragic drama, with its more strenuous and problematical assertion of control, can make endurable again. Short of this concentrated sublimity of tone and effect, the sublimity of Aeschylus or Racine, or of Shakespeare at his tragic climaxes, the possibilities of the first-person mode seem inexhaustible.

II

The Melvillean narrator acts and is acted upon, being a character in his own recital. (Indeed in the five books before *Moby-Dick* there are scarcely any other developed characters; there are only sketches, types, more or less distinctive examples of the conditions of life being described.) But more especially he *tells*—recalls, considers, meditates, emphasizes, explains. He acts, that is, primarily in his formal role, coming to life through his own narrative voice. A certain degree of absorbed passivity and reflective detachment marks off the Melvillean narrator from the Romantic hero of passion and energy or from the type of the quester after experience. His character, as recording witness, is to remain radically open to experience without being radically changed by it; he is to identify and judge matters without equivocation, yet not show himself too overridingly anxious to impose his outlook upon them. In this respect the part he plays goes according to the arch-Romantic conception of the poet or artist—the conception of the creative intelligence as the agent of a "negative capability," the source of whose power is in the free and sympathetic readiness of its responses to the phenomena of life. Thus, the role given the narrator in Melville's chronicles is determined, we may say, not only by the situation and actions being rendered but by the very job of rendering them. Certainly Melville used his narrators to convey his own thought and feeling; what should be emphasized is that he was at the same time subjecting his reckless personal bent toward declamatory self-expression to the formal discipline of a naturally suitable working method.

This reserved freedom of response in Melville's narrators, and the corresponding rhythm of their absorption and detachment, is what sets them apart as moral agents in his fiction. They are not made to claim any greater power over their lives' conditions than is granted any one else. The intuition that "to treat of human actions is to deal wholly with second causes" applies to them as well. Yet there is a difference, which shows first in the simple mechanics of the first-person mode as Melville used it. Though the narrator will speak of his own behavior deterministically and see himself as at any given moment fate-dogged and nearly powerless, the very fact that he is not only describing the events of the narrative from another point in time but taking just as much time as he needs and wants in order to recall them makes for a certain actual freedom from them and equanimity about them. The business of retrospective narration presumes, and creates, its own detachment, its own independence, its own (as we like to say of Ishmael and his admirable breed) "survival." So Ishmael's qualities—his unflagging readiness, bluff stoicism, impartial mockery, sensuous sympathy, and intellectual vivacity, all maintained in the face of the most fearful omens, and strongly counterpointing Ahab's madness—do not make their impression on us in the book as a dramatic model and triumph of exemplary character. What they do directly refer us to is just that art of which they are the means and first effects, the convention-rooted art by which the book as we have it has been created. The rare congeniality of the narrator (i.e., of his voice) marks, formally, the creative fulfillment of this narrative genre Melville had steadily been working in, and is the first sign of his mastery in *Moby-Dick*.

Melville had an impressive flair, as a writer, for direct, unmediated assertion, but when he attempted to make it the whole basis and instrument of his exposition, as in *Pierre*, it could go outrageously to waste. In *Moby-Dick*, on the other hand, the plain procedures of narrative recollection, the tangible gathering up of past events into the present sequences of a recital, are the means, practically, of his success; through them the most prodigious and terrific phenomena are subdued to the masterable logic of human time and human understanding. All other characters in the book exist only within the action of the story, and are wholly subject, as we see them, to its course of happenings. The narrator, however, exists to tell the whole story out, and therefore moves above it and around it, as well as through it, in relative freedom. The result is that the leading gestures of the work as a whole, and the pattern of experience displayed in it, are never quite the same as what its staged events add up to—or would add up to if presented dramatically only. At least a double focus is established; we see things as they are in the immediate passion of human effort, but also as they appear to detached observation in the mere succession of their occurrence.

What is thus added by the refractions of first-person narrative does rub off, of course, upon the character of the presenting "I." He may well come to epitomize in himself, so far as he has a definable self, the attitude and outlook of the whole work. In Melville's handling, though, he remains most interesting as he holds to his primary role, and even retires a little behind it. That is, he serves better as observer and commentator than as controlling actor. The one book, *Mardi,* in which Melville gave his narrator the really determining role in the action is his weakest in this mode. It is not just that "Taji" is most of the time "a disembodied spirit telling a disembodied story" (as Edward Rosenberry has accurately remarked); it is rather that making the narrative voice the main agent and motivating source of the events which are to be chronicled seems to forfeit some necessary margin of discursive freedom.

The case is otherwise with the first-person narrators used by Poe, and the difference is worth examining briefly. The "I" of Poe's psychodramas is always rather strictly characterized. As a person he must positively complement, when he does not himself embody, that concentrated passion or impulse which it is Poe's purpose to put on display as shockingly as possible—and Poe understood that the form and the voice, more than the material details, are what set the intensity of the shock. The adventures through which this display is made are usually more or less fantastic. They are closet-adventures, and the whole point of the way in which they are manipulated is (in W. H. Auden's words) "to prevent the reader from ever being reminded of historical existence" and "real people." [3] By contrast Melville's purpose is precisely to display this real world, or some real (however exotic) part of it, from the perspective of attitudes natural to it. Except for *Mardi* all his first-person chronicles are abundantly documentary, in a strict sense. And the presence of the narrator is most vividly felt when he is most occupied with the presentation of actual facts and conditions. He may express anger or contempt or despair at what he sees in the world, but he takes this world as he finds it, and indeed

[3] "Introduction," *Selected Prose and Poetry of Edgar Allan Poe* (New York, 1950), p. vi.

discovers his voice in describing it; this is the primary task he keeps himself free for—and he gains a verifying identity insofar as he carries this task through.

For such writing the freedom of maneuver of the first-person voice is of critical importance. Its advantages, however, Melville did not begin to exploit really artfully until *Redburn* and *White-Jacket*.[4] In both of these we find the narrator easily adapting his address to the affair of the moment without losing plausibility as a concrete person—managing widely different tones and postures; showing off an insider's mastery of his special business, then securing the wider point of view by cross-references to other kinds of experience and other men's thoughts; holding together all the while the sequences of short, quickly varied, impressionistic paragraph-jottings that in these books Melville largely relies upon for exposition; and speaking in the main as though to an audience of good fellows of liberal curiosity like himself, who might go where he goes and would see pretty much as he sees. In all this he combines both ends of one of the classic experiences in nineteenth-century fiction, the experience of entering the great world and getting an education by it; he embraces both the raw natural educability of the young apprentice to life and that versatile moral intelligence of the finished man which is the proper outcome of the whole process. With Melville's narrators that process does not happen to be the main theme. His books (*Pierre* apart) are not the romances of education that now and then they seem on the point of becoming. But our confidence in the documented account of the state of certain worldly matters, which is Melville's prime concern, is doubly secured by the impression we get of the intervening narrator's own reflective sophistication. His chronicle may charm us by renewing the freshness of first discoveries, but it gains its authority by consistently judging things (so Cesare

[4] Melville's disparagement of these two books was perhaps an oblique recognition of this very artfulness, as viewed from the Romantic standard of confessional sincerity.

Pavese described the effect) "with the calm certainty of the man who has *studied*." He has not just encountered this fact and learned that truth. He has rather grown into a permanent readiness of imagination: a responsiveness so alive and earnest as to corroborate the particular data of remembered sensations while at the same time gaining acceptance for his furthest effort to identify and explain them. With such an interlocutor we begin to feel that no divination is impossible, that nothing essential will be left obscure or unassimilated—and thus a formal anticipation, that in due course what has been undertaken will be completed, is established as effectively as by any ingenuities of dramatic organization. So long as the narrative maintains this liberality of address, it continually prepares its own further way.

The young freeborn gentleman-adventurer, sympathetic, versatile, unprejudiced, curious, meditative: this is one of two main character-types Melville used for his narrators. The other is the mellowed old hearty who holds the floor in "Bartleby," "Jimmy Rose," and "I and My Chimney." Again the type is sentimentally appealing, as Melville meant it to be. But the simple combination it presents of tolerance, whimsy, acceptance of things-as-they-are, and obduracy only over a few inoffensive private comforts and preferences, would not be enough to sustain interest through forty or fifty pages without some more active virtue; and this again is the genial heartiness and humor of response that we find recorded in the quick pace and free movement of the recital itself. Melville never worked more adroitly than in "Bartleby" and "I and My Chimney," which are both charmingly executed yet teasingly profound and moving in implication, and full of the sharp turns and recoveries of wit.[5]

[5] In "Bartleby" it is in fact the elderly narrator's quick humor that releases the important secondary action of the story—the helpless movement of his own sympathy toward the "motionless" scrivener and his acceptance, against all natural disposition, of a personal "mission" to serve Bartleby in his withdrawal out of the world.

The moral type of both narrators, the young rover and the old hearty, is broadly the same, granted the difference in age, and is one of Melville's most distinctive creations. Their voices make no false appeal for our attention. They are as easy and just in substantiating commonplaces as in confronting the strange and rare. In behavior they follow unconstrainedly the leadings of impulse without surrendering their freedom as observers and interpreters. In a world that normally makes a mockery of the reductions of ideologies, and of interpretive formulas and logical imperatives, they are, in a modest way, of the special party of the "uncompromised"—one proof of this being their power of sympathy for the representatives of that "choice hidden handful of the Divine Inert" who so tantalized Melville's moral imagination, and whose presumed character contrasts so sharply with the passionate willfulness of an Ahab or a Pierre. They have our trust, these narrators, and rarely abuse it.

III

Melville's particular skill in handling first-person narration may be illustrated by a comparison of two well-known passages from the American "classics," the first chapter of *Moby-Dick* and the first chapter of Washington Irving's *Sketch-Book* ("The Author's Account of Himself"). Their similarity goes well beyond their introductory function. In each the effort is to establish the speaker in the character of the restless romantic voyager; and each moves directly on, as quotation will show, to essentially the same corroborative image or scene, as well as to the implicit suggestion that the feelings described are such as any man of sense would experience in the same circumstances. Here is Irving's Geoffrey Crayon:

"This rambling propensity strengthened with my years. Books of voyages and travels became my passion, and in devouring their contents, I neglected the regular exercises of the school. How wistfully would I wander about the pier-heads in fine weather, and watch the parting ships, bound to distant climes;

with what longing eyes would I gaze after their lessening sails, and waft myself in imagination to the ends of the earth!

"Further reading and thinking, though they brought this vague inclination into more reasonable bounds, only served to make it more decided. I visited various parts of my own country; and had I been merely a lover of fine scenery, I should have felt little desire to seek elsewhere its gratification, for on no country have the charms of nature been more prodigally lavished. Her mighty lakes, like oceans of liquid silver; her mountains, with their bright aërial tints; her valleys, teeming with wild fertility; her tremendous cataracts, thundering in their solitudes; her boundless plains, waving with spontaneous verdure; her broad deep rivers, rolling in solemn silence to the ocean; her trackless forests, where vegetation puts forth all its magnificence; her skies, kindling with the magic of summer clouds and glorious sunshine; no, never need an American look beyond his own country for the sublime and beautiful of natural scenery.

"But Europe held forth the charms of storied and poetical association. . . ."

And here is Melville's Ishmael (who has already, in the book's opening paragraph, begun to turn attention off himself and his private reasons for going to sea):

"There now is your insular city of the Manhattoes, belted round by wharves as Indian isles by coral reefs—commerce surrounds it with her surf. Right and left, the streets take you waterward. Its extreme down-town is the battery, where that noble mole is washed by waves, and cooled by breezes, which a few hours previous were out of sight of land. Look at the crowds of water-gazers there.

"Circumambulate the city of a dreamy Sabbath afternoon. Go from Corlears Hook to Coenties Slip, and from thence, by Whitehall, northward. What do you see?—Posted like silent sentinels all around the town stand thousands upon thousands of mortal men fixed in ocean reveries. Some leaning against the spiles; some seated upon the pier-heads; some looking over the bulwarks of ships from China; some high aloft in the rigging, as if striving to get a still better seaward peep. But these are all landsmen; of week days pent up in lath and plaster—tied to counters, nailed to benches, clinched to desks. How then is this? Are the green fields gone? What do they here?

"But look! here come more crowds, pacing straight for the water. . . ."

The differences of treatment and effect are obvious, and there is no great point in dwelling on them—or in belaboring Irving's inert rhetoric with sentences produced by Melville at the top of his form, in quite another kind of book, a critical thirty years later. But the contrast does point up the special abruptness and boldness with which, in *Moby-Dick,* the openings toward both audience and material are followed up. No sooner does Ishmael establish his personal character, in the first chapter, than he transforms it into a dramatic pose and promptly disappears into that. He makes his reader a positive accomplice —there now is *your* city, the streets take *you* waterward—the more effectively through the succession of commands and questions that follows: look, go, what do you see, why is it so, but look again! The device is transparent, and possibly risks impudence. What carries it off is the energetic particularity of the speaker's harangue, his quick attentiveness not only to "you" but to "them" and "it." The reader is caught up in specific names and images. The tour he is peremptorily summoned to go on is through concrete things, places, and events, with alternate possibilities. "Confidential" is from the first the word for Ishmael, but what is confided is not only a personal attitude but objective fact, observation, incident, aspect, enveloping condition.[6] Without some such enthusiastic projection of self into

[6] In a sense this style extends to the reader the generous ideality of Melville's treatment of all phenomena. By speaking as if everyone in his hearing must share his own natural vitality and spirit, and his uninhibited involvement in a vital world of experience, the narrator positively transmits these lively virtues to his actual audience. Thus it is that works of literature make themselves "useful" to us.

material circumstances, this cheery familiarity of address would merely be impertinent and would cloy. It would have no natural function of disclosure, and we might well find ourselves preferring, over the long haul, the less overbearing company of a Geoffrey Crayon.

Characteristically, for Melville, the passage quoted proves itself most forcefully at its descriptive climaxes—in the exact kinesthetic hyperbole of "nailed to benches, clinched to desks," and in the expanding sympathy that builds to the image of landsmen mounting the rigging in their voiceless excitement. The note sounded, the gestures caught, are typical of Ishmael's witness. He is always something more than a figure of certain propensities and tastes who invites us to follow him around as he exercises them. He appears rather as a man attended—by "fate," he tells us; by a certain recklessness of inward temper; more decisively, as the teller of the story, by a capacity for being wholly absorbed into the images of his recollection. He does not stand on any private dignity. The range of his qualities is genuinely appealing: gaiety, compassion, a quick pleasure in the odd and the picturesque, a deeper elation of spirit in the presence of the really strange, a zest for sharing his enthusiasms (and for defining them), a self-awareness that is reassuringly self-deprecating, and then gusto, flippancy, gravity, sincerity, or awe, as the occasion warrants. As an observer and commentator he is discriminatingly alert to the way things happen in the world and especially to the conduct of men in it—an instance is the masterly series of sketches of the *Pequod's* mates (Chapters 26–27) and how each goes about his mortally hazardous work. As a chronicler of the adventure and the technology of whaling he holds easily to the human scale, yet he does not sentimentalize; he is as precisely sensitive to the "momentousness" of individual persons, including other writers, as to those "slidings and collidings of Matter" that Lawrence praised him for apprehending. Perhaps nothing is more ingratiating in Ishmael than the respectfulness of his appeal to older authorities—voyagers, chroniclers, scholars—in filling out his long narrative. We notice his interest, especially, in the testimony of "exact and reliable men"; it is as one such that he would wish himself to be known.

But these personal virtues of Ishmael's are really incidental to the imagination and voice, the authenticating turn of style, that sustain the whole bulky structure of *Moby-Dick*. For all the variety of the effects achieved, voice and style are consistent throughout the discursive mass of the book. They are fundamentally the same for its "larger, darker, deeper" concerns as for its representations of material fact. The standard of the "exact and reliable" holds for both kinds of exposition. It can sometimes make for rather elaborately adjectival writing, but even the most prodigal sequences of modifiers usually show a logic of conception as well as of sound and cadence. "A *wild, mystical, sympathetical* feeling was in me," Ishmael declares, in pledging himself to Ahab's purpose—and in due course devotes two magnificently detailed chapters, "Moby Dick" and "The Whiteness of the Whale," to confirming the simple accuracy of these high-flown epithets.

A sure instinct for when to hurry and when to take his time, for quick transition and for patient elaboration, is a major resource in Melville's art of spoken narrative. More than anything else, I think, it is his masterful control of the *pace* of Ishmael's exposition that secures for the narration in *Moby-Dick* the direct, continuing accent of reality. Chapter after chapter acts out rhetorically the conscious imaginative possession of what is there to be told. In writing of the emblematic Bulkington, for example, Ishmael does more than describe and represent; halfway along he positively rushes out to join him, as if to encourage the man in the behavior that makes him notable, as if he were real and alive and once more at that special parting of the ways marked out for him, and as if perceiving this about him suddenly enabled one to speak from an even further penetration into the whole "mortally intolerable truth" of things. ("Know ye now, Bulkington? Glimpses do ye seem to see . . . ?") Of this control of the pace of disclosure and confirmation, this capacity to reproduce in meditative recollection the compounding rhythm of the whole conceived experience, the last paragraph of the important sixteenth chapter, "The Ship," provides another fine example. It comes just after Ishmael, now signed on for the *Pequod's* voyage but somewhat apprehensive about what is to come, has been absorbing from old Peleg a particularly wild barrage of hints and warnings concerning the ship's mysterious captain:

"As I walked away, I was full of thoughtfulness; what had been incidentally revealed to me of Captain Ahab, filled me with a certain wild vagueness of painfulness concerning him. And somehow, at the time, I felt a sympathy and a sorrow for him, but for I don't know what, unless it was the cruel loss of his leg. And yet I also felt a strange awe of him; but that sort of awe, which I cannot at all describe, was not exactly awe; I do not know what it was. But I felt it; and it did not disincline me towards him; though I felt impatience at what seemed like mystery in him, so imperfectly as he was known to me then. However, my thoughts were at length carried in other directions, so that for the present dark Ahab slipped my mind."

In such passages, in which the sequence of emotion in time past is given to us through the intense reflective emotion of the narrator's present—its strong pulse marked off by the short phrases and clauses, each built on one or two defining words—the truth and the sufficiency of Ishmael's dramatic witness are not to be doubted. Yet we notice that there is no special appeal here to an established *character* in the speaker. The appeal is firmly to the quality of the event, and to the feeling of the moment. Ishmael's progressive withdrawal as a distinct character into the impersonal business of narration, a formal phenomenon which has bothered not a few of the book's critics, is only a step further, and a step that seems to me very efficiently prepared. Without these cultivated artifices of the first-person method, Melville's triumph in *Moby-Dick* is, strictly speaking, unimaginable.[7]

[7] Since writing this chapter I have been pleased to find a concurring defense of Melville's narrative method in Professor Glauco Cambon's spirited article, "Ishmael and the Problem of Formal Discontinuities in *Moby-Dick*," *Modern Language Notes*, LXXVI (June 1961), 516–523. Professor Cambon develops his argument in terms of the structure of the book, which he sees as "dialectical" in its modulations of voice and point of view (rather more deliberately and conscientiously so than seems to me the case with so obviously extemporized a performance), and for which he cites classical precedent. The narrative discontinuities, so he puts it, are "the structural equivalents of the copious hyperboles which animate Melville's baroque prose."

CHAPTER SIX

MELVILLE'S STORY-TELLING

> "There is no difference between this art of story-telling, this art of making words, lines, sentences, and images follow one another, of explaining something once without allusions or subtleties, calling wine, wine, and bread, bread, and this ancient art of weaving, this art of making threads and colors follow one another in a neat, clean and orderly fashion. First you see the stalk of the rose, then the petal, then the crown; but we all know it's going to be a rose from the beginning."—SILONE, *Fontamara* (tr. Harvey Fergusson II)

SOME IDEAL fulfillment in form of the long documentary-confessional first-person narrative may perhaps be imagined, but Melville never stayed to achieve it. Various transient motives diffuse the effort of composition in all his early books. Their vivacity and earnestness of voice catch our attention easily enough, but do not greatly concentrate it or build upon it; there is little of the intense consolidation of effect that we feel working in a rigorously developed art. Even *Moby-Dick* labors somewhat through this kind of diffuseness. One would hesitate to pick out any one chapter or emphasis in it as expendable, yet clearly the recital by Ishmael and the drama of Ahab do not hang perfectly together.

Toward the middle of *Moby-Dick*, however, we come all at once upon what was for Melville a new formal experiment in the writing of fiction; and the remarkable thing is that we find him mastering the form involved at the first try, and with a conspicuously free and easy originality of treatment. "The Town-Ho's Story" (Chapter 54) is of course consistent in manner of presentation with the rest of the book. Ishmael remains the narrator in his own superintending person, and his tale fits expertly into the larger scheme, giving us for one thing an impressive forewarning of the white whale's actual power without dissipating the suspense of the *Pequod's* long search. Nevertheless this interlude is different in kind not only from the narrative it interrupts but from anything else in Melville's earlier writing. It is a rounded piece of pure story-telling, with beginning, middle, and end, in which a whole single action is rendered with a correspondingly whole postulation of its interest and meaning. Once again, it is true, a narrator presents himself as intermediary. But he is not this time an active participant in the events of the story. His part is rather to tell it as it has come down to him, and to explain its details or confirm their probability as his immediate audience requires him to. But to do this is in fact to renew the story's existence in human consciousness *as* a story, which is to say, as a particular (and, in method, familiar) formalization of recollected events, and thus as the agency of their acceptance and continuance in common discourse.

The narrative form involved, a new one for Melville, was no novelty to his public. On the contrary it was perhaps the most popular literary form of the day in the United States. And it is to be distinguished from the genre of the traveler's chronicle Melville had thus far been exploiting precisely in the degree of technical sophistication it had undergone by 1850, and in the maturity of its proved conventions. Nothing had a surer acceptance on the literary market, and nothing could provide a surer basis for improvisation and experiment, than the picturesque anecdote or tale of emotion-fraught adventure, with or without an idealized moral significance. Those few that are still read—the stories of Irving, Poe, and Hawthorne, or tours de force like "The Big Bear of Arkansas" and, some years later, "Jim Smiley and his Jumping Frog"—are what remain of a vast outpouring of magazine and newspaper work in this vein, among the more assiduous producers of which were the New York "Knickerbocker" writers of the generation between Irving and Melville. The originality of "The Town-Ho's Story" shows rather in the apparently instantaneous freedom and adroitness of the author's handling of this popular mode, and in his turning it to his own uses and bringing it off so effectively at a single try.

Measured against the mass of *Moby-Dick*, "The Town-Ho's Story" is a modest achievement. But it is also as convincing a sign as an alert contemporary would yet have encountered of Melville's authority as a writer of fiction. For here, in submitting his talent for the first time to the conventions of as well-established and technically advanced a literary genre as then existed for his use, Melville for the first time produced a technically finished and self-contained work of narrative invention. In structure it conforms to the popular "frame" technique of story-telling, the occasion of the telling being used at the beginning and end to set off the main line of action. This in fact is just where Melville's easy competence is most immediately evident. The setting of the Golden Inn at Lima, friends lounging on the piazza in the evening over *chicha* and cigars, is picturesque in itself, as well as being naturally suitable to the telling of stories. At several points in the recital Melville brings Ishmael's audience of cavaliers back into view, using their gravely attentive reactions to support the tone and point up certain colorful details, and to ratify the strangeness and excitement of the story's wilder passages. But the back-and-forth of these interruptions could seem mechanical as a device if it did not also work to somewhat subtler ends. The fact is that our attention is being directed along two courses at once. There is the material action, certain reported events featuring certain remarkable characters. But there is also the formal gathering of these events and characters into recollection and some order of imaginative understanding. The very fact that they are met with in what is announced as a story is the first and the decisive step in this process of assimilation; from the beginning the supposition must be that the events will lead in sequence to a definite termination and that the characters' part in them will have been made at least outwardly intelligible. Thus the dramatic suspense of the story's action is substantially modified by the logic of the form. It must partly give way to suspense of a different kind—the formal suspense of hearing a familiar kind of discourse through to its proper end, and a promised series of events to an identifying conclusion.

For the teller, in such a tale, there is presumably no dramatic suspense at all.[1] He knows from the first where the sequence he is rehearsing will end (though he does not necessarily know what it means), and this foreknowledge must influence his way of presenting it. To a corresponding degree it will influence our response. The effect of the teller's peculiar intercession upon the stuff of his story will be matched, more or less controlledly, by the developing curve of the hearer's expectation and readiness. Something like this happens of course in any presentational art; the point is that with the told story this correspondence may very naturally become a main part of the formal mechanism of the work. So often as we are referred back to the occasion of the telling, by just so much our attention will be displaced from the events narrated to their subsequent emergence, through the narration, into the general currency of human understanding. The ebb and flow of the narrator's recital, now following the action at close quarters and now standing off to comment and speculate, co-operate to the same broad result. In the case of "The Town-Ho's Story" the dramatized presence of the listening cavaliers substantially increases this displacement. So in various ways we are made witness not only to the bygone conflict of a Steelkilt and a Radney but to the survival of this conflict as a factor in continuing human apprehension—just as in *Moby-Dick* as a whole

[1] Compare Poe's first-person tales, which do not often overcome the serious handicap—to our taste—of the teller's over-insisting that there *is*, and that he is all but overwhelmed by it.

we are absorbed equally into the lively grandeur of the prime materials and into the corresponding largesse of Ishmael's rendering of them.

The story itself (as distinct from its substance though not independent of that, and as the perceptible means of this transmutation or liberation of raw experience) may thus become the writer's object, or para-object—and it is no small part of Melville's delivered "meaning" in this interlude-chapter to let us see that the telling of such a story exacts its toll. Ishmael is shown as considerably exhausting himself in his effort to exert and renew his story-teller's authority over experience. At the end we see him wound up to the pitch, literally, of swearing to the truth of his recital, for which he now feels a grave personal responsibility ("this your story," the courteous Don Sebastian has said, without sarcasm), and of superfluously risking blasphemy by calling for priest and Book to swear by. It is fair to add that the story itself is worthy of this second climax. By some standards it may not appear a proper story at all, for the denouement is accidental and not a dramatic consequence of the conflict of its characters: the revenge Steelkilt plans to take upon Radney is arbitrarily accomplished by Moby Dick. But as Ishmael tells it, I should argue, it is wholly coherent, and wholly absorbing. In the clarity of its motives and forces, the grandeur of its setting, the poetic reasonableness of its rugged justice, it is indeed "passing wonderful." Its main occurrences have, in their smaller compass, the prodigal vivacity and excitement of all of *Moby-Dick*. And the whole performance seems as characteristic an expression as anything else in that extraordinary book of the author's great technical gifts—his nimbleness and inquisitive thoroughness in primary exposition, and his deliberate artistic honesty in following through to the end the openings of imagination.

"The Town-Ho's Story" was in fact first put into print a month before the publication of *Moby-Dick*—in *Harper's New Monthly* for October 1851. Except for a few early reviews and newspaper squibs and for the occasional printing, after publication, of excerpts from his earlier books, this was Melville's first venture on the market which was to occupy him almost exclusively during the second phase of his short public career. In changing, after *Pierre*, from a writer of books to a writer for the magazines, Melville met with a success no less immediate than he had enjoyed as the author of *Typee* and, if anything, rather more consistent. To a businessman-of-letters like G. W. Curtis, then reading for *Putnam's Monthly*, work by Herman Melville was no longer an automatically saleable commodity, but had in each instance to prove itself; nevertheless, everything Melville submitted to *Putnam's* and *Harper's* between 1853 and 1856 was promptly accepted with the single exception of the "Two Temples" sketches, refused "reluctantly" by *Putnam's* as possibly giving offense to "some of our church readers." In volume, this magazine work is scarcely less, year by year, than what he had produced before *Moby-Dick*. In variety of theme and invention and in technical control, it seems to me distinctly superior. If by some sad chance Melville had survived to us only in the stories and sketches of this brief period, there would still have been high excitement at his recovery as a serious writer, and we would still rate him one of the few accomplished craftsmen in our nineteenth-century prose fiction, at least the equal of Poe and only a little less of a master than Hawthorne.[2]

[2] Here is the chronology of Melville's work during these years:

1853. November–December—"Bartleby the Scrivener," *Putnam's*, two instalments.
December—"Cock-a-Doodle-Doo!" *Harper's*.
1854. March–April–May—"The Encantadas," *Putnam's*, three instalments.
April—"The Two Temples" submitted to *Putnam's*.
June—"Poor Man's Pudding and Rich Man's Crumbs," *Harper's*.
July—"The Happy Failure," *Harper's*.
July 1854 to March 1855—"Israel Potter," *Putnam's*, nine instalments.
August—"The Lightning-Rod Man," *Putnam's*.
September—"The Fiddler," *Harper's*.
1855. April—"The Paradise of Bachelors and The Tartarus of Maids," *Harper's*.
April—"Benito Cereno" submitted to *Putnam's*, published in three instalments, October–November–December.

II

1. In turning to the form of the told story, Melville was committing his talents and energies as a writer to one of the classic modes of prose fiction. The measure of his accomplishment between *Pierre* and *The Confidence-Man* is in the manner of his performance within this mode, and in his realization of its formal possibilities. That there are such formal possibilities, the management of which is a matter of importance to criticism and to the understanding of literary "tradition," seems obvious enough; one should not have to insist that story-telling is an art requiring an exact imagination and capable of the most serious uses, and that the conventions and effects peculiar to it are worth trying to understand.

Yet the drift of much recent critical discussion of the novel has been, in effect, to deny these truisms; to raise a certain conception of dramatic organization as an absolute standard of value for fiction; and to dismiss the told story, along with related forms like the recital and chronicle, as necessarily inferior, a kind of sub-art. This attitude seriously warps, for example, the otherwise admirable essay by R. P. Blackmur on "The Craft of Herman Melville" (1938), which still stands out as a uniquely stimulating inquiry into the actual character of Melville's performance as a writer.[3] Blackmur's judgment is (or was) unequivocal: Melville's work "nowhere showed conspicuous mastery of the formal devices of fiction which he used," and

---

May or June—"The Bell-Tower" submitted to *Putnam's*, published in August.

July—"I and My Chimney" submitted to *Putnam's*, published in March 1856.

November—"Jimmy Rose," *Harper's*.

1856. January or February—"The Piazza," written to introduce *The Piazza Tales*, published in May by Dix & Edwards.

March—"The 'Gees," *Harper's*.

May—"The Apple-Tree Table," *Harper's*.

October—a contract settled with Dix & Edwards for publication of *The Confidence-Man*, Melville sailed for Europe.

[3] *Virginia Quarterly*, xiv, 266–282; reprinted in *The Lion and the Honeycomb* (New York, 1955).

therefore it neither had nor could have any influence on the general art of fiction, since "there was nothing formally organized enough in his work to imitate or modify or perfect." Blackmur was not indifferent, it should be added, to the virtues of Melville's prose. He defined them indeed with great care, observing that Melville "habitually used words greatly," and that his was a "great" style insofar as it maintained on many levels and for many purposes "the qualities of accurate and objective feeling." But the larger arts of construction, the securing formal "strategies" by which the significant novelist will reveal himself, lay, for various irreversible causes, beyond his reach. Hence he was a writer of rare genius who could not bring off a satisfactory whole performance, who showed greatness but "added nothing to the novel as a form."

Unhappily the evidence Blackmur used to fill out this forthright argument is drawn largely from *Pierre*—though surely the chief lesson concerning forms, and "strategies," which that overwrought book has to teach is that a writer even of the first rank working under disabling personal strain may abuse the best and worst of them indiscriminately. The argument, however, does not really depend on the example chosen. What Blackmur mainly objected to is present in one way or another in everything Melville wrote. It is, in brief, his way of directing the progress of his story in his own person, of commenting on it editorially or chorically, and, in the process, of stating his themes "not only baldly in isolation, but out of place and rootlessly." Blackmur remarked that while such interpolations are often magnificent in their kind, it is just their kind which is distracting, since they work "outside the story." Now this of course should be a matter for observation; we either do or do not find it happening, and the work as a whole suffers or gains accordingly. But Blackmur's judgment was categorical: a novelist's interpolated commentary, when it attempts to be rhetorically self-sufficing as Melville's consistently does, *cannot* find place and root in his story. "A dramatist," Blackmur wrote, commenting on the splendid passage in Chapter 16 of *Moby-Dick* in which the type of Ahab's heroism is broadly foretold, "would have been compelled to find the sentiment of these sentences in a situation, an action, and they could have been used only as the situation called for them and the action carried them along; and *a novelist when he can should follow the example of the dramatist*. Melville preferred the non-dramatic mode." [4]

So indeed he did—and would come to grief, as Blackmur points out, precisely when, as in *Pierre*, he went against this preference. But what shall we say of the rule put forward here? Our concern is no longer simply with Melville's special practice but with the general logic and art of prose fiction, and the question must be asked: is it true that dramatization is the only possible mode of composition for the serious narrative artist? Surely not—though certain neo-Jamesian fundamentalists have thought so. The history of the novel suggests otherwise, and not least, it is worth pointing out, the history of the novel in the twentieth century, the novel of Joyce, Lawrence, Mann, Kafka, Proust, Gide, Faulkner, Virginia Woolf, Silone; this more recent history might well be written in terms of a steady and radical withdrawal from the strictly dramatic model.[5] Dramatic organization after all is not a categorical necessity but an elected method of composition. Like any method of composition (as Gertrude Stein recognized) it is a method of *explanation*, of setting things out and exhibiting their properties. As

[4] Italics mine. The problem here is in part, though only in part, a problem of vocabulary. One may sympathize strongly with Northrop Frye's insistence on reserving the word "novel" for one particular class of prose fiction, yet still follow the convenient usage of applying this word to any fictional narrative in prose and of a certain length. This freer usage may indeed have positive advantages—it may at least help to frustrate dogmatically restrictive views as to what properly belongs in the "house of fiction."

[5] So, too, the books that seem to me the masterpieces, each according to its intention, of the lean decade of the 1950's—*Dr. Zhivago, The Leopard, The Fall, The Music of Time*—are all episodic, anecdotal, and expository in method, and dramatically diffuse in the extreme.

a way of deploying the materials of a story it is an artifice, a convention (and for the novel, of course, a borrowed one); and it is dependent like any artifice or convention both on the competence of those using it and the acceptance of those invited to pay attention to it. The method of narrative description and commentary, I am saying, is another such convention. It calls, I think, for at least an equal compositional skill, and it can be the occasion for quite as prodigious a display of inventiveness and imaginative truth. Certainly it requires no greater allowances on the part of the reader, no more radical a suspension of disbelief, than does the pretence, on the printed page, of dramatic immediacy and completeness. For the dramatized novel builds on a speculative premise that will not in itself bear very close scrutiny—the premise that the "real" order of phenomenal events will be revealed to us if only we take the trouble to observe those events thoroughly enough, and that it is satisfactory in representing human affairs to show causes directly and coherently touching their effects. The cult of the wholly dramatized novel, more especially the dogmatic formal theory deriving from it, represents, one might argue, a curiously protracted last stand in literary criticism of doctrines of philosophy, and in particular of verifiability, which have not been seriously entertained in their own right since the labors of Hume and Kant in the eighteenth century.

Like any fictional form, a dramatic demonstration must be contrived and superintended, and it must prove its fitness to its uses. At the least it must ring true, psychologically, morally, and with respect to the frame of manners and social usage within which it is set. What more, exactly, need be asked of the freer conventions of story-telling? The value of any sort of statement in fiction, however it is developed, depends on the wit and force, the sense of fact and equally the sense of proportion and relevance, of the writer delivering it. If, interceding in his own voice upon the material action, he can make his intercession count in one way or another, if he is ready to take positive advantage of what is actually a multiplication of his formal openings, there need be no loss of intensity or diffusion of effect. Rather, there may be a real extension of imaginative authority, as the core of action is overlaid by the analogies of free speculation. As with the first-person chronicle, the story-teller's mediating presence may thus take on its own kind of demonstrative interest. Intelligence and control make all the difference. What seems a technical fault in a Thackeray or a Meredith may be essential virtue in a Stendhal, a Conrad, a Tolstoy, a Melville—or in a Flaubert, telling us openly at the last crisis that it is prostitution poor Emma Bovary has descended to. The method can especially serve those writers, that is, whose power of statement is not only representational. When the interpolations are obtrusive, one is likely indeed to find that they say less, not more, than is manifest in the pretended action. The fault then is in the writer, not in the method *per se*.

2. The distinction we need is between two broad modes of exposition in fiction. In English we struggle along without efficient names for these two modes, and our ordinary criticism of the novel is so much the poorer. French usage, on the other hand, at least roughly indicates them by the terms *roman* and *récit*, and it is in two passages of modern French criticism that I find the best description of their fundamental qualities and differences. In an essay, significantly, on Proust—who wrote the greatest of modern novels by making simultaneous and profoundly creative use of both—Valéry defined the difference between them in terms of the end each has in view.[6] The generally dramatic mode of the *roman* attempts to create "the illusion of having lived, strenuously or deeply, through a discrete action" (in which respect, Valéry shrewdly observed, it formally approaches the condition of dream). The generally expository mode of the *récit* attempts to create another kind of illusion, that of the "precise knowledge" of such particulars as it may disclose. Each lives by conforming to one absolute law,

[6] "Hommage à Proust," *Variété I* (Paris, 1924), pp. 157–165.

which is that the projected sequence of disclosure carry us along, even absorb us, into its particular compositional end, its produced effect. And with regard to expressive power and authority, Valéry suggested, there is really nothing to choose between them; he was in fact so caught up by the case for equal standing he was making for the *récit* that he felt obliged to deny the necessity of downgrading the *roman* as a result of it.

The second passage, in an essay by Ramon Fernandez on the method of Balzac—the master of the nineteenth century in fiction as Proust is of the twentieth—takes its cue from just these definitions of Valéry's, which it cites, however, for the purpose of disputing the critical theory implicit in them.[7] The supreme effect in fiction, Fernandez predicates, is dramatic immediacy, and the great advantage of the *roman* over the *récit* is precisely its command of this effect. What mainly distinguishes the two modes is that "the event of the novel *takes place*," as in a vital present, "whereas that of the recital *has taken place*" and is now withdrawn from actual time and space into an abstract order of idea, or of recollection. More fully: "The novel is the representation of events which take place in time, a representation submitted to the conditions of apparition and development of these events.—The recital is the presentation of events which have taken place, and of which the reproduction is regulated by the narrator in conformity with the laws of exposition and persuasion."

As a statement of how the two modes operate, this can hardly be improved upon. It only does not prove what Fernandez meant it to, and needs therefore to be detached from his insistence on the necessary superiority of the *roman*, the work of "spontaneous and immediate evocation." For as he expands his account of the *récit* he continues to make nothing but the most remarkable claims for it. As a mode of presentation, he writes, it approaches "on the one hand to reasoning and the intellec-

[7] "The Method of Balzac: The Recital, and the Aesthetics of the Novel," *Messages*, tr. Montgomery Belgion (New York, 1927), pp. 59–78.

tual laws of combination, and on the other hand to painting and the general laws of description." Exactly what more than this need be said in defense of any art? The events of life, their "conditions of apparition and development," are in truth what they are known as, through description and through reasoning; and an art that manages to deliver an ordered knowledge of them, according to the mind's experience of discovering the conceivable manner of their existence, will not be less significant or less "real" than an art that presumes to imitate their raw falling out. We know that immediate experience is never wholly intelligible nor exactly translatable. The direct rehearsal of it in art requires of us an extraordinary credulity. The finest master cannot carry us with him unless the way has been prepared by some sort of rational reckoning, a priori, of the phenomena of experience—their customary behavior, their probable arrangement, the probable significance of the impressions they cause. In the arts, forms are the agency of this reckoning, and the great artist invariably presents himself as a renewer of forms—which in turn prove to be wonderful conservators of knowledge and sensibility. The convention of dramatic re-creation is one such form, one such prepared way of comprehending experience. The convention of the recital, or told story, is another, expressing a somewhat different understanding of particular events. It is a way, in fact, of getting at all those aspects of reality which the foreshortenings of dramatization may blur or black out altogether. And if indeed it can avail itself (according to Fernandez' formulation) of the general method of both philosophical reasoning and representational painting, then it makes possible a penetration into reality of the utmost subtlety and seriousness.

The special virtue of the told story, I have been suggesting, is in its doubled focus—on the event, and on the recapturing of it; on the particular phenomena of experience, and on their participation in the volatile continuum of human life and understanding. As a form it takes risks, as any form must. Even if the tendency to diffusion rather than concentration of effect is overcome, there may be a disconcerting brokenness and anti-climax in the serial action. The free observation of motive and feeling in the individual characters may be constricted. There may be a superficial indifference to the ordinary, familiar evidences of personality and personal relationships. These defects (if they are such) result in turn from the major sacrifice the form makes, which is to give up the illusion of direct engagement with the body of experience. (But it may be taken as a sign of health that the told story does not have to depend on reproducing life, or mimetically competing with it, in order to make a significant response to it.) What is gained by way of compensation is considerable. As the method of story-telling rehearses the recollection, in their known sequence, of events which have already reached some termination, it is peculiarly equipped to suggest the special dimension of the *historical* in passing reality, and therefore to contribute the more effectively to the ceaseless redefinition and renewal of what has already come to pass, through the corporate human effort of living toward the future. Its discontinuities and anti-climaxes give it in fact something of the ruggedness of recorded history, in which most of what actually happened is obscured or lost yet significant actions may be traced out. Correspondingly, too, it may take on something of the excitement of prophecy, the predicated future being indistinct only in the detail.

Thus, like both historical chronicle and word-of-mouth folktale, the form of the narrated story can provide a vivid paradigm of the irregular capacity of men for collective, and recollective, self-consciousness. Open-ended, working often by ellipsis and by silences, naturally hospitable to merest hints and unproved analogies, it freely invites the reader's connivance; it trusts his patience and his thoughtfulness, the capacity of his responses for biding their time, his power to keep the shape of one thing in mind until another turns up to reinforce it. So the justness of its exhibitions will often be less a distinctly moral than a poetic or metaphysical justness, alive to the deeper logic of causality and succession—and requiring, incidentally, no casual effort of attention. For what, finally, this method of narration may be said to aim at is nothing short of a renewal (for told stories are always to be told again) of mankind's way of communicating with itself, of keeping track of its behavior and the conditions of that behavior, across space and the barriers of circumstance, and through time and the barriers of oblivion. So it may perform the invaluable function of reproducing for contemplation—as the novelist Michel Butor has suggested—the fundamental form and manner of our common apprehension of things.[8]

3. In one manifestation or another—anecdote, exemplary tale, synoptic life-history—the genre of the told story has been dominant in American fiction, from the work of Brockden Brown and Washington Irving to that of Sherwood Anderson, Faulkner, and Fitzgerald, James Thurber and Eudora Welty, *Nine Stories* and *Pigeon Feathers;* and the question occurs, how is this formal bias to be accounted for? Various answers have been suggested, by writers as well as by their critics. The stricter formal structures of novel and drama, it has been argued, require a more settled social order, and more firmly established social norms and values, than have ever yet materialized in the United States. The fluidity of individual lives combined with the sameness of their opportunities, the superficial diversity and underlying monotony of personal existence in America, have been adduced, as throwing interest back upon such abstract patterns of behavior as any life or action traced to its end, in the predictable succession of its stages, can be counted on to display. There is also the argument from style or voice:

[8] The recital, M. Butor writes, "est un phénomène qui dépasse considerablement le domaine de la littérature; il est un des constituents essentiels de notre appréhension de la réalité. Jusqu'à notre mort, et depuis que nous comprenons des paroles, nous sommes perpétuellement entourés de récits, dans notre famille tout d'abord, puis à l'école, puis à travers les rencontres et les lectures." ("Le Roman Comme Recherche," *Répertoire*, Paris, 1960, pp. 7–11.)

to those for whom the climax of American literary development has been the capture of household and regional vernaculars for literary use, the genre of the told story appears as the natural instrument in prose of this technical exploit, corresponding to the monologues of a Frost, a Pound, a Williams, a Robert Lowell, in poetry.

All such hypotheses are worth considering, even for the limited purpose of accounting for Melville's prompt mastery of the story-telling mode. What I should like now to stress, though, is the logic of the mode itself. Specifically, what it presumes, and more or less strictly enforces, is a direct collaboration between the teller and his audience. For the duration of the telling each is privileged to exist by the story's quickening grace: each asserts a real existence by his assent to the occasion; each confirms his own real presence in contact with the other's. And of the fiction that formally results, may not at least this much be said, that whatever its other merits it seems a deeply characteristic mode of expression for an open and equalitarian society? For in the ritual encounter of these otherwise featureless and traceless persons—the one telling his story of what he has seen or done or heard about; the other giving credit to it and therefore not only to the teller's identity but to his own as well—do we not have a model of free social intercourse in a libertarian democracy, where each man tends at once to a unitary freedom and to interchangeableness and anonymity? Correspondingly, do we not also have a prime instance of the ceremonies of communion to which the popular arts and popular imagination in such a society instinctively reach out? However wishful, however fantastic, however abortive in its continuances, news of each other's lives is what we want to hear. Let two or three Americans gather together, and these mysterious social truths will declare themselves. That is why serious conversation in the United States is so insistently anecdotal, an exchange of retrospective monologues, and so vague and dispiriting when it attempts any freer function. And that is why

American writing so often turns on the special pathos of isolation and unfulfillment when one man's experience or vision of things, his husbanded testimony, is not such as anyone else knows how to share.

Just this situation, this profoundly democratic pathos, is addressed in Melville's poignant tale of John Marr—a fine example on a small scale of his ability to secure effects of great resonance without benefit of dramatic elaboration and climax. An old sailor, widowed and childless, is described living out his once free-and-easy life far inland among farm people, people who are presented as earnest and decent but barely capable of the most casual sociability; and he finds himself unable to establish any other relation with them than "that mere work-a-day bond arising from participation in the same outward hardships": "At a corn-husking, their least grave of gatherings, did the lone-hearted mariner seek to divert his own thoughts from sadness, and in some degree interest theirs, by adverting to aught removed from the crosses and trials of their personal surroundings, naturally enough he would slide into some marine story or picture, but would soon recoil upon himself and be silent, finding no encouragement to proceed. Upon one such occasion an elderly man—a blacksmith, and at Sunday gatherings an earnest exhorter—honestly said to him, 'Friend, we know nothing of that here.' "

III

A painstaking casualness of exposition distinguishes all the stories and sketches Melville wrote between 1853 and 1856. Events are reported as they have fallen out, to observation or general hearsay; at the same time there is a continual pressure toward catching them up at once in some summary definition. The rhythm of the recital alternates accordingly between the quick pace of immediate happenings and the slower fluctuations of the teller's progress toward an understanding of them. One or the other rhythm may dominate. So "Bartleby," which runs more to dialogue and an orderly progression of incident, is only a little removed from an essentially dramatic organization; whereas in "Benito Cereno" for nearly a fifth of the text the narrative is wholly superseded by extracts from the record of a court trial that belongs to the story but takes place quite outside its frame of action. These radical shifts of narrative pace and perspective, these interruptions for comment or for validating evidence, are also present in Melville's first several books; but there, where his purposes were descriptive and documentary, they do not seem out of keeping with the general scheme of presentation. For the different purposes of the novella or tale, they are usually felt to be much less suitable. To as sympathetic a reader as Newton Arvin they are simply further indications of Melville's "flagging vitality and depleted inventiveness" in the years after *Moby-Dick;* they are so many obstacles to what was really needed, "a clear and strong perfection of fictional form." [9] My own view of the workmanship in Melville's later stories (and of the standard of "fictional form") is rather different, as must now be fairly clear. In any case it seems only reasonable not to write off so persistent a set of compositional practices as the product of exhaustion or fumbling, but to take them as they come, for the serious virtue that may be in them; for what they positively contribute, that is, to a body of work of which it is scarcely possible not to feel the peculiar originality and expressiveness.

The uneasiness of critics with Melville's narrative procedures has been especially acute in the case of "Benito Cereno." [10]

[9] Arvin, *op. cit.*, pp. 231–240.

[10] Disagreements about this story tend to be complete, but arise, I think, largely from misconceptions as to the form adopted and the effects proper to it. For various reasons there is a reluctance nowadays to accept Melville as first of all a teller of stories. A work of literature that resists reductive "interpretation," and that primarily intends to rehearse a certain circumstantial course of action, seems somewhat less than wholly serious. The "gray shadows" of those high-minded Puritan forefathers whose dismissal for frivolity Hawthorne pretended to fear are still among us, disguised as interpretive critics, and it is their habit to be ill at ease with imaginative literature until it has been tidied up for value-analysis and tricked out to

Here, in point of fact, he was retelling an old story, the central situation and many details of which he had come upon in a *Narrative of Voyages and Travels in the Northern and Southern Hemispheres* (1817) by one Amasa Delano—whose name he did not bother to change. What was it that attracted Melville to this story, in which an odd and vaguely ominous succession of incidents is suddenly revealed, in a single instant of action, to mean very terribly the opposite of what it has seemed? If we take Melville's rendering of it as a fable—of innocence and evil, or of spiritual obtuseness and spiritual suffering—we might indeed have to say that the narrative is awkward and negligent in composition, and that it really does not make its point. Surely a competent allegorist could have managed the display more efficiently, and a clear-headed moralist would have devised a less eccentric balance of forces. But is it not reasonably apparent that what primarily caught Melville's practical interest as a writer was just the intense chiaroscuro strangeness of the situation and of its material facts, with their—literally—double

---

resemble those decorous humanistic fables or shadow-plays (or paragons of "fictional form") preferred by general-educators and their helpless students.

In any case, consider these two representative views of "Benito Cereno." To Richard Chase it is "masterful," both in building up dramatic suspense and in its resolution of certain unitary "moral ideas." To Newton Arvin, however, it is an "artistic miscarriage," written at too low a pitch to signify much of anything. The difference of opinion seems absolute. Yet both views, we notice as we follow them out, proceed from the assumption that the story is to be understood as a *parable*, a methodically figurative display of, in this instance, the exposure of something called "innocence" to something called "evil" or "the dark side of life." And by applying to it, arbitrarily it seems to me, the standards of allegorical or of dramatic coherence, both commentators—Chase not less than Arvin—miss the particular logic and fascination of this remarkable narrative. The earlier impressions set down by John Freeman and Yvor Winters seem to me much more responsive to Melville's actual accomplishment—the first finding in the story's "broken and oblique narration" a perfected anticipation of a method dear to Conrad; the second categorizing it as the portrayal of an *action* and its effects, in a style ("the style of a novelist") which is "both classical and austere" in going about its appointed business.

See Richard Chase, "Introduction," *Selected Tales and Poems by Herman Melville* (New York, 1950); Newton Arvin, *Herman Melville* (New York, 1950); John Freeman, *Herman Melville* (New York, 1926); Yvor Winters, *Maule's Curse* (Norfolk, 1938).

meaning? Why else should he stick so closely to the data of his source, and set the additional incidents of his own invention in so nearly the same mold? Melville's leading impulse in working out the sequence of his retelling was to capitalize on just this material ambiguity, and on the delayed double-exposure it results in. That impulse was not greatly different from the conjuror's impulse behind those stories of Poe's (also written for magazines) which are exercises in the fine art of mystification. The appearances put before us in "Benito Cereno" constitute a riddle, and the business of two thirds of the narrative is the elaboration of this riddle and then its sudden clarification (thus the climax is no more a dramatic one than the climax of Poe's "The Gold-Bug").

Of course there is "more" to the story than this—a moral gravity, a psychological intensity, an appropriately shadowy atmosphere, an ironic realization of the stain of human slavery. All these things Melville drew out of his materials, and they have not gone unnoticed. But one way of appreciating his achievement in "Benito Cereno" is to see how all this "more" is built directly upon the central ambiguity, the mechanism of mystification. What we are shown comes largely by way of Captain Delano, through what he notices about the strange Spanish ship and its stranger captain and through what he progressively thinks—or gets almost to the point of thinking. At the end, it is true, the contrast between Captain Delano's awareness and Don Benito's rather displaces the riddle through which we have come to know it. Yet there is no real effort to harden this contrast into a generalized moral figure. It is presented simply as the consistent outcome of the harrowingly different circumstances through which these two lives have come to their strange meeting. "Benito Cereno" does have, I am sure, a seriousness of general implication and a closeness to common reality that reach beyond Poe's capacity as an artist. By its strict narrative fidelity to its particular core of truth, certain features of it are indeed powerfully suggestive of some general order of existence. The states of mind Captain Delano passes through are not, after all, essentially different from the ordinary ways by which we move, more or less blindly, through our works and days. So the story can fairly be seen as composing a paradigm of the secret ambiguity of appearances—an old theme with Melville—and, more particularly, a paradigm of the inward life of ordinary consciousness, with all its mysterious shifts, penetrations, and side-slippings, in a world in which this ambiguity of appearances is the baffling norm. But to say this of "Benito Cereno" is precisely not to lose sight of its form as a story, and of the curious way in which the exposition is actually carried out.

There remains the problem of the ending. The event clearing up the stretched-out riddle—Don Benito's leap, and then Babo's after him, into Captain Delano's whaleboat—takes barely a page and a half to describe; a few more pages quickly close out the main action of the story. But then everything that has happened so far is put before us a second time, and more besides—in the cumbersome style of a judicial exposition (modeled on documents given in the source narrative). Other than that it fills pages, is there anything to be said for this contrivance? Or do we concur in the judgment of the story's first reader, the knowledgeable G. W. Curtis, who told the editor of *Putnam's*: "It is a great pity he did not work it up as a connected tale instead of putting in the dreary documents at the end.—They should have been made part of the substance of the story."

No doubt an argument on the point of form which is involved can be made either way. My own judgment of the matter begins simply with my finding this part of the narrative exactly as interesting as the mystifying incidents which it follows and which it serves to review and explain. If we take "Benito Cereno" as allegory or fable, these court documents must seem a mistake, and a nearly inexplicable mistake. If our measure is dramatic organization, they are scarcely less troublesome. But if we accept it as, in form, an extended narrative riddle, then they are legitimate, or make themselves so. We are not finished with a serious riddle when we hear it solved. It remains to go back over all the significant detail of it from the point of view of the revealed solution. For both the riddler and (if he has been played with fairly) the beriddled, this orderly itemization of data which was first mystifying but now falls into place rounds out the pleasure given by the whole performance. And in this respect the riddle may be seen as a particular, highly stylized variety of the general form of the told story. Hearing a story which holds our attention to its promised end, we are similarly reluctant to let go. We look ahead to retellings. We circle back through the cruxes and important details; perhaps we imagine new details to heighten its special effects. And then we have somewhat to exorcise its charm over us, and our indulgence of that. We must allow the mechanism of our encounter with it to run down, to trail off into "anti-climax"; so we act to contain its disturbing force. The more concentrated the story, the greater the need to relax its hold gradually. For as it has the mettle and integrity of its own purposes, and stands by its own manner of assertion, it will the more compellingly gather to itself (as already in the imagination of its teller) reflections, afterthoughts, analogies, all those gestures of bemusement by which we acknowledge any efficient display of things-in-sequence. For all this to happen, of course, there must be in its readers a free play of curiosity and a willingness to be forcibly entertained. That is, there must be a positive tolerance of story-telling (as of anecdote and gossip) as a main type of the familiar music of civilized discourse—not always useful, not always harmonious. But those capable of this tolerance have their reward.

Actually, in "Benito Cereno," the introduction of explanatory documents is only the most abrupt of a series of shifts and starts in the presentation, roughly corresponding to the developing import of this curious story. The ambiguities of the riddle are acted out by a rapid alternation of moods, at once in the general atmosphere and in Captain Delano's mind. The compositional device that particularly sustains this pattern of alternation is the fragmenting of much of the narrative into very short paragraphs, a great many of which are just a sentence long and barely consecutive. A typical example is this passage following up the episode in which the negro Babo, after shaving Don Benito, whines that he has been punished with a razor cut for inadvertently scratching his master's cheek:

"'. . . Ah, ah, ah,' holding his hand to his face.

"Is it possible, thought Captain Delano; was it to wreak in private his Spanish spite against this poor friend of his, that Don Benito, by his sullen manner, impelled me to withdraw? Ah, this slavery breeds ugly passions in man.—Poor fellow!

"He was about to speak in sympathy to the negro, but with a timid reluctance he now re-entered the cuddy.

"Presently master and man came forth; Don Benito leaning on his servant as if nothing had happened.

"But a sort of love-quarrel, after all, thought Captain Delano.

"He accosted Don Benito, and they walked slowly together. . . ."

The very spareness and (emphasized by the paragraphing) brokenness of this kind of exposition are central to the story's massed effect—the sense of tension increasing and diminishing, the irregular measuring out of time, the nervous succession of antithetical feelings and intuitions. But once the riddle is broken open and fairly explained, once our concern can go out at last to the passional outcome of the whole affair, a different tactic is in order. So on the last page of the story we find Melville spinning out the same kind of spare, rapid, matter-of-fact statement into longer paragraphs and a more sustained and concentrated emphasis:

"As for the black—whose brain, not body, had schemed and led the revolt, with the plot—his slight frame, inadequate to that which it held, had at once yielded to the superior muscular strength of his captor, in the boat. Seeing all was over, he uttered no sound, and could not be forced to. His aspect seemed to say, since I cannot do deeds, I will not speak words. Put in irons in the hold, with the rest, he was carried to Lima. During the passage, Don Benito did not visit him. Nor then, nor at any time after, would he look at him. Before the tribunal he refused. When pressed by the judges he fainted. On the testimony of the sailors alone rested the legal identity of Babo.

"Some months after, dragged to the gibbet at the tail of a mule, the black met his voiceless end. The body was burned to ashes; but for many days, the head, that hive of subtlety, fixed on a pole in the Plaza, met, unabashed, the gaze of the whites; and across the Plaza looked towards St. Bartholomew's church, in whose vaults slept then, as now, the recovered bones of Aranda: and across the Rimac bridge looked towards the monastery, on Mount Agonia without; where, three months after being dismissed by the court, Benito Cereno, borne on the bier, did, indeed, follow his leader."

Especially after the teasing oscillations of mood in the long first part and the dry repetitions of the court records that follow, these fine last paragraphs, terse, rapid, taut with detail, seem a particularly impressive instance of Melville's ordinary boldness in fitting his performance to the whole developing occasion. There is no worked-up climax; what is said is shaped strictly to the job of making an end. Other instances, from other work, may be cited. *Moby-Dick* especially is alive with this matching of narrative pace and address to the matter in hand—as in the series of paragraph breaks and openings at the beginning of the splendid chapter, "Brit," coming just after three static expository chapters of whaling lore:

"Steering north-eastward from the Crozetts, we fell in with vast meadows of brit, the minute, yellow substance, upon which the Right Whale largely feeds. For leagues and leagues it undulated round us, so that we seemed to be sailing through boundless fields of ripe and golden wheat.

"On the second day, numbers of Right Whales were seen, who, secure from the attack of a Sperm Whaler like the Pequod, with open jaws sluggishly swam through the brit, which, adhering to the fringing fibres of that wondrous Venetian blind in their mouths, was in that manner separated from the water that escaped at the lip.

"As morning mowers, who side by side slowly and seethingly advance their scythes through the long wet grass of marshy meads; even so these monsters swam, making a strange, grassy, cutting sound; and leaving behind them endless swaths of blue upon the yellow sea.

"But it was only the sound they made as they parted the brit which at all reminded one of mowers. Seen from the mast-heads. . . ."
—so we keep pace as the *Pequod* is borne deeper and deeper into the marvelous arena of its fated voyage.

Once gained, this sensitivity in handling narrative became for Melville—especially after the drawing-in of his ambition as a declarer of prophetic truths—perhaps the steadiest of his working motives, and the surest source of his unflagging originality. In the closing chapters of *Billy Budd* we find the same deliberate use as in "Benito Cereno" of an interrupted, anti-climactic descent from the main line of action, for the sake of a further climax and consolidation of feeling. At another point in *Billy Budd* a curtain of silence and secrecy is abruptly brought down, in the middle of the thickly circumstantial narration, as a means of setting off the pivotal episode of Vere's last interview with Billy. A similar interruption figures at the center of the eighth "Encantadas" sketch, in the story of the Chola widow ("Against my own purposes a pause descends upon me here"); again, what lies deepest in the story is as if handed back to the imagination of the reader—for whom, of course, the teller's abrupt gesture of reticence is as effective as any dramatic image.

In each case, we see, the effect is managed with a perfect

simplicity of means. And it is in this free control of narrative succession, this precise formal response to his story's advancing power of implication, that we find the central compositional tact of Melville's art. It seems to me a creative tact of the very highest order.[11] At his level best he will not force his tales out of their advancing line of truth—not for the sake of a a moral argument, nor for dramatic sensation, nor for any preconceived formality of design. He is indeed, in managing his materials, the least arbitrary of the great American writers—which is one reason, I think, why his work as a writer of stories seems to move the most insistently and yet naturally toward the free suggestiveness, the profounder creativity, of myth.

[11] Is it not what is disturbingly absent, by contrast, at too many critical junctures in Henry James's more intricately designed and (as Gide accurately put it) *dominated* novels and stories? There is too little margin, in James's fiction, for exploiting the purchase gained by the painstaking efficiency of the form and the fluid intelligence of the style.

CHAPTER SEVEN

WORDS, SENTENCES, PARAGRAPHS, CHAPTERS

> "His work is a whole and he is everywhere true to himself."—PASTERNAK, "Translating Shakespeare"

BETWEEN *Typee* and *Moby-Dick* Melville's signature distinctly emerges, out of the welter of the styles and expressive modes he was coincidentally learning to manage. This aspect of his achievement is unmistakable. We take it to be a sure mark of his literary mastery. But it is rather easier to recognize than to define. For by "signature" I mean something more at least than a certain pattern of mannerisms recurring with a certain frequency—as I mean something other, for example, than (in the case of Melville) that resourceful "idiosyncrasy" of diction itemized by Newton Arvin for *Moby-Dick*. I mean, rather, a consistent impress of consolidation that registers in every dimension of the writer's work and that compels our attention not because it produces this or that meritorious effect or serves this or that expressive task but because it contrives its own autonomous figures of statement and forces us to reckon with them on any spectrum of understanding we commit ourselves to at all seriously. For the writer this signature becomes part of the governing logic, perhaps the main part, of all the forms and conventions he employs. It justifies these forms and these conventions and renews the life in them; it becomes, in a way, their reason for being. Thus it results not so much in any specific tactics of expression as in a kind of fullness and finality of consideration—or so the reader has reason to feel. The matter in hand has been seen through to an end; we sense that we have come upon the last word.

In the writer's maturity his ordinary working idiom may continue to change and to change remarkably—as Melville's does with *Pierre* and again with the varied work of 1853–1856. He may contrive any number of new departures. Yet as his writing maintains some part of its mastered freedom and power of imagination, his signature will remain. It strikes us, once we are aware of it, as the essential instrument of his creative authority. It acts to complete the imaginative circuit, sealing the mechanism of the composed work into a certain uniformly directed energy of statement. Thus it will always seem as much a force of mind, a pressure of intelligence and imagination, as a perfection of craft or technique. But of course some steady competence of craft and technique is required for it to register at all, and for the contexts in which it can operate to be solidly established.

The assumption in this four-part chapter is that Melville is a master of expression, whose writing gives pleasure and secures its effects by a persistent variety and resourcefulness of technical performance, but whose greatness as a writer is in this further impress of consolidation, which is at once formal and intellectual. Precisely because this impress is felt at every significant point, however, what exactly it consists in can only be suggested rather abstractly. One can simply cite certain passages, the proper whole contexts of which are too long to be reproduced for demonstration. I apologize therefore for the fragmentariness of the argument that follows—which is scarcely more than a listing of admired examples—and must leave confirmation to the interested reader's own deliberated judgment.

I

The diction and idiom that gain for *Moby-Dick* its exceptional animation of style are sensitively analyzed in Newton

Arvin's excellent study of the form of Melville's masterpiece.[1] Arvin describes two features in particular: first, that "verbal palette" of favorite words and epithets through which major themes are developed and an appropriate atmosphere conjured up; second, the coinages, the improvisations, the transpositions of parts of speech (verb-nouns and noun-adverbs, participial modifiers, pluralized substantives, adjective-compounds, and so on), by which Melville regularly quickens his presentation. Arvin's efficient tabulation does not need to be repeated here. It may be considerably supplemented, however. The "dark" cluster of words Arvin noted as characteristic of the book's expressive vocabulary—"wild," "moody," "mystic," "subtle," "wondrous," "nameless," "intense," "malicious," and their cognates—is only a partial accounting. A quite different tone-cluster may quickly be identified, conveying an equally important set of impressions and themes: "calm," "fair," "mild," "serene," "tranquil," "cool" and "indifferent" (for behavior), "noble," "grand," "lovely," "heavenly," and so forth. Typically, such words appear in contrasted pairs—"joy" and "woe," "wolfish" and "soothing"—a practice helping to anchor the book's idealizing propensity in the ambiguities of actual feeling and actual experience.

But it is not just this kind of bold emotional coloring that Melville's epithets work toward. Words for states of feeling are matched in frequency by words for the generic forms and root conditions of things, or for the relations between things and their encounters with human perception. "Dim" and "indefinite" are two such (so the *Pequod* in its death-throes is seen "through dim, bewildering mediums"); indeed the commonest descriptive adjectives take on something of this generalizing power when used in support of categorical noun-abstractions. In the same vein we hear of a "desolate vacuity

[1] *Herman Melville,* pp. 162–165. See also the essay by Jean-Jacques Mayoux, "La Langue et le Style de Melville," *Vivants Piliers: Le Roman Anglo-Saxon et les Symboles* (*Lettres Nouvelles* 6, Paris, 1960).

of life" or simply of "the half-known life"—the phrases seem to hint at some universal law in the particulars they speak for.[2] Certain other words in constant use neither describe nor categorize any specific objects or feelings. Rather, set out among the book's superabundant vocabulary for objects and feelings, they assert a defining frame within which these are to be felt as acting—thus, "world," "earth" and "earthly," "all," "mortal," and the like—or, like the emphatic modifiers "wilful" and "deliberate," they particularize certain ways of happening rooted both in human character and in the surrounding temper and habit of universal nature. It is Melville's genius to make these risky abstractions seem as concrete as his directly sensuous or kinesthetic language. And it is the coordination of these two vocabularies, the sensuous and the categorical, involving the transposition of the values of each to the other, that especially renews, in reading *Moby-Dick*, our confidence in the book's profoundest imaginative effort, its search after some ideal apprehension of both the natural existence of things and the active convulsions by which each thing participates in that existence.

The choice of words is primarily a function of the image-making power, and thus too of the underlying sense, and conception, of reality. Their placing and timing, on the other hand, is more strictly a matter of rhetoric, and in a prose writer of the first rank will reveal at least an equal wit and inventiveness. The narrative of *Moby-Dick* abounds in rhetorical manipulation of the most provocative sort; and though the units of effectiveness are more often the larger ones of sentence, paragraph, and chapter, some instances of an essentially rhetorical use of the single word or phrase deserve mention in this brief

[2] Words of this sort, indicating whole categories and systems of phenomena, are among the principal instruments of Melville's expressive authority. Their definiteness, and their frequency, suggest that some prime effort of interrogation is irrepressibly going forward through the act of writing, and that nothing really significant is going to be slighted.

survey. Exaggerated repetition of some otherwise unremarkable word is a common enforcing device with Melville—for example, "old" (with various synonyms) in the paragraph in Chapter 16 describing the *Pequod,* or "savage" in Chapter 57, concerning the virtue of patient industry in men. Usually this kind of repetition, as with Dickens and Carlyle, is for a comic or a polemical effect, but it may also serve a graver expressive purpose, as in the series "pitiable," "pity," "pitied," and "piteous" in the long account in Chapter 81 of running down an old, blind, stricken bullwhale. There is frequent use, too, of archaism and of colloquial irregularity, carrying always a risk of affectation but usually contributing some valid local emphasis. Unexpected adjective-noun combinations are another typical device: in Chapter 26 the phrase, "concentrating brow," clinches a significant premonition of the characteristic personal energy of Ahab, while a few lines later the phrase, "immaculate manliness," intensifies the idea of that common democratic heroism in Starbuck and his kind which it will be the narrator's sorrowful task to show overthrown.

But it is difficult to suggest out of context the effectiveness of even these few and simple instances.[3] And it is next to impossible to do justice, in a hit-and-run fashion, to those verbal inventions in *Moby-Dick* which do not so much create yet another vivid picture or image as provide a stirring musical accompaniment for the ritual procession of all its pictures and images into our concentrated attention. To be led, in discussing a book's vocabulary, into consideration of effects of this kind

[3] The force and definiteness of language in *Moby-Dick* are so continuous that to pick out a scattering of examples can misrepresent the actual running effectiveness of the narrative style. The commonest descriptive sequence may also display this creative energy. Note the plain nouns and verbs and the one odd adverb in the following paragraph, showing us Ahab as in the intensity of his single purpose he impulsively forswears smoking: "He tossed the still lighted pipe into the sea. The fire hissed in the waves; the same instant the ship shot by the bubble the sinking pipe made. With slouched hat, Ahab lurchingly paced the planks."

is to begin to discover in just what way its style is inseparable from its general apprehension of things—at which point the most determined analysis of the writer's art falls hopelessly behind his actual inventiveness. One other characteristic operation of individual words in *Moby-Dick* should be mentioned, however, and that is Melville's way of calling attention through a single epithet to the whole sustaining form of his story and so of reinforcing, in the middle of some lively local context, the largest expectations already established. Typically his instrument for this effect is the participial modifier. "Preluding" is one such ("so still and subdued and yet somehow preluding was all the scene . . ."); "foreshadowing" is another ("In this foreshadowing interval . . ."); and both serve, like the corresponding series of epithets applied to the fatefully advancing ship, to support the whole precariously extended and delayed structure of the narrative.

A main part of our critical interest in Melville's books before *Moby-Dick* is in watching this expressive vocabulary forming and taking hold. So we pay special attention to the vivid, tensile language of certain passages in *Redburn* and *White-Jacket;* more than the rhapsodizing of *Mardi* these carry, we feel, the promise of their great sequel. A capacity for strong emotional coloring, an alertness to the resonance of the right names of things, a facility with metaphor, a natural command of prose cadence, and simply that plenitude and resourcefulness of diction which is Melville's least debatable merit as a writer—all are intermittently active in these two books just preceding *Moby-Dick,* and tend on the whole to gain in effective mass as each narrative goes forward. Following the ordinary romanticism of his era in prose, Melville started as primarily an expressionistic writer, a transmitter of salient aspects; and therefore it is less the affective energy of his language than its increasing solidity and explicitness that marks, for us, the emergent master. The first quality was in the contemporary romantic fashion; the second he had not only to achieve for himself but to learn to want to achieve.[4]

In the sparer style of Melville's prose after *Moby-Dick* and *Pierre,* individual words and phrases are less conspicuously thrust forward. They seem less exploratory, less (literally) provocative. We feel that Melville is no longer so consistently following their lead into the possible meanings and openings-out of the material in hand. Except as part of a general effort toward exact definition, the diction in this later work does not attract attention to itself. The distinction of the language is now a distinction of controlling intelligence, of right judgment and completed understanding. Single words are still potent—"penal" and "penitential" in "The Encantadas," along with the suggestive concreteness of "clinker" and "scar" as names for that blighted landscape; or the superb epithet "motionless" for the first appearance of Bartleby; or the whole rather stiff and angular vocabulary of specification in *The Confidence-Man* and *Billy Budd*—but they serve more to crystallize governing impressions than to search out new meanings. They function now like signals; like "apparitions," as Professor Mayoux nicely describes them; like standing mirrors of the realities they denote. The effort is simply to be precise, to give right names. A language of denomination, it might be called, and it has its

[4] A practical sensitivity to the properties of particular words seems present in Melville's work from the first, and underlies all its further development. In *Typee* this virtue is applied pleasantly enough to the job of tone-coloring and picture-making. But it is *Omoo,* I think, with its more casually sufficient diction, that more distinctly presages the objective tact and competence of Melville's maturer style. One incidental sign of this is the liberal use of shipboard vernacular for ordinary exposition—though the author feels obliged to segregate it a little by means of quotation marks. In the opening pages we find "hove to," "ship" (as an intransitive verb), "bunk," "small stores," and "creating a sensation," all hedged typographically but not really apologized for.

We may note too how some of the "verbal palette" Arvin identifies in *Moby-Dick* is already in conscious use in *Omoo*—in the first chapter we find "melancholy" and "strangeness" pointedly focusing attention, and a moment later a fine spotting of participial modifiers in the phrase, "patched and blistered hull." But there is not yet the prolonged building up of complex tonal combinations in the service of a leading theme.

own perils. When some right word or determinative name is not forthcoming, a kind of ponderous stuttering can set in—as in the first long paragraph of Chapter 5 of *The Confidence-Man,* with its proliferation of "may" and "might" and "seemed" and "appeared" and "perhaps" and "sometimes" and "not wholly" and "seldom very," without one firm verb or noun. Scrupulousness of that sort is likely to be self-defeating, even for a writer with great and grave things to say. There is always some use, stylistically speaking, in a capacity for small talk. But the instance is a freakish one; it is not for the most part in matters of language that *The Confidence-Man* falls short of its highest promise.

II

What Albert Thibaudet said of Proust—that the tide of his sentences indivisibly bears with it as it advances the creative élan that gives it life[5]—is true in some measure of every greatly original writer. The unit of the sentence is as a generative cell in which the writer's effort repeatedly renews its peculiar prerogative. And it is perhaps the making of successive sentences, the continuous syntactical propulsion of the writer's utterance, period upon period, that most insistently tests his working mettle and determines his acceptance with his readers.

What makes for good sentences is as hard to specify as any aspect of literary form. Here especially the ordinary separation of form and content, for convenience in argument and under cover of the truism that they are of course inseparable, breaks down entirely. No doubt various sound principles of evaluation can be formulated. At the least it will be agreed that no mere "ingenuity of varying structure"—as Robert Frost once put it—can hold attention for long, can "save prose from itself."[6] A test of fitness applies: fitness to the subject and to the whole

[5] "Marcel Proust et la Tradition Française," *Nouvelle Revue Française,* xx (January 1923), 130–139.

[6] Preface to *A Way Out* (New York, 1929).

expressive occasion (but the sentences themselves articulate the subject and compose the occasion); fitness also to the natural character of the language (which lives only as such constant renewals keep it alive and in working order).

Can we say simply that those are good sentences, establishing a good style, which are most responsive to the nature of the performance they are a part of, as in their succession they build it up? For the Melville of *Moby-Dick*—a confident and effusive, yet restlessly speculative and interrogating writer, engaged upon a composition the whole grand design of which was apparently open to radical adjustment down almost to the completion of it—very different sentences, performing different local functions, will stand out, and not only those that most emphatically declare the book's major themes and accents. We are struck, in turn, by certain descriptive periods rich in sensuous and pictorial detail or vividly alert to the pressure and pace of physical events, by the teasingly conjectural aphorisms on the mysteriousness of phenomenal appearances, by the spectacular flourishes of completion with which various key paragraphs and chapters are wound up, and so on. Other general types of sentence may be identified; every reader of Melville will have his own favorite examples. But as in the case of individual words and phrases, to draw up a list of fine sentences in *Moby-Dick* is to misrepresent the nature of Melville's stylistic achievement, the real distinction of which is that it is nearly continuous throughout the long, packed narrative. The significant proof of his mastery of the sentence in this book, and in the best of his later writing, is that it operates at the level of ordinary workmanship.[7]

[7] Only with dialogue, in *Moby-Dick*, does it seriously falter, in misguided efforts at a theatrical excitement and sonority, or in attempts to communicate simultaneously a character's immediate passion and the objective condition of being that underlies it. Then we get the self-parody and plain awkwardness of a declaration like the following, spoken by Ahab: "What is best let alone, that accursed thing is not always what least allures." Or from pious Starbuck: "Let faith oust fact; let fancy oust memory; I look deep down and do believe." Or from Ahab again: "In

A routine sentence opening Chapter 45, "The Affidavit," is a case in point. Characteristically it makes a full paragraph. It directly follows an intense and splendidly executed rhetorical climax in the chapter preceding and takes the form of a comment and apology about the whole shifting narrative enterprise as that now stands and is about to be renewed: "So far as what there may be of narrative in this book; and indeed, as indirectly touching one or two very interesting and curious particulars in the habits of sperm whales, the foregoing chapter, in its earlier part, is as important a one as will be found in this volume; but the leading matter of it [i.e., extraordinary evidences of the regular behavior of whales] requires to be still further and more familiarly enlarged upon, in order to be adequately understood, and moreover to take away any incredulity which a profound ignorance of the entire subject may induce in some minds, as to the natural verity of the main points of this affair." Sentences of this quality do not seem likely, on the face of it, to enhance a writer's reputation for style. The writing is audibly labored, as in the awkward terminal succession, "in this book," "in this volume," "of this affair." And though some flatness (irregular grammar apart) is expectable—given the job of resuming the exposition after the wrought-up passage just completed—it is not all to be explained away as a

---

the midst of the personified impersonal, a personality stands here." Such sentences usually, as it happens, are meant to convey important meanings, and regularly serve as cruxes of critical interpretation. But that of course does not justify them. Rather, it tends to cast some doubt back upon the writer's fundamental seriousness—not to speak of the critic's who builds his argument upon them.

It is not that Melville could not write dialogue, or could only write it for low or comic characters. The swift, serious exchange between Ahab and Captain Gardiner of the *Rachel*, for instance, is admirably done, and contributes solidly to the final tension of the chase. It is rather that for the high declamatory soliloquies, mostly given to Ahab, he was unable to find, or to improvise, any viable prose convention—or else was kept from devising one by his temporary fascination with Shakespearean models—though his management of the same materials, same insights, same range of reference, same vocabulary of specification, in Ishmael's explanatory narrative is by contrast adroit, natural, and consistently graceful.

calculated effect or as something formally necessary. That this sentence has a more positive value, however, is not hard to show. It is clearly more than a mechanical connective—or, as Melville works it out, it presses to become so. It begins by acknowledging, and at an appropriate point, the peculiar design of this most peculiar book ("So far as what there may be of a narrative . . ."); it then directs attention to the relative importance of the matters immediately in view and to the manner ("indirectly touching") of their relationship to the suspense-shrouded main action; also, it keeps track of the reader's reactions, or that one reaction ("incredulity") which *must* be forestalled, and contributes to the forestalling by setting the narrator's promise to explain these matters "still further and more familiarly" over against the "profound ignorance" of "some" hearers; finally, it specifies a standard ("natural verity") by which both matter and manner are properly to be judged. In short, it performs real work; and its modest whole effect, launching us upon a new chapter, is at least momentarily to confirm our confidence in the general scheme of the book and in the writer's readiness to carry it forward in an intelligible and interesting way.

The test of such sentences is whether they do carry the freightage packed into them without interrupting the sequences they fill out. Melville's desire for thoroughness of treatment seems on the whole to increase as his books accumulate, and results eventually in the casual tortuousness and heaviness of much of his later prose. The sentence-making in *The Confidence-Man* and *Billy Budd,* in particular, is of this nature. Increasingly he seems to build each new syntactical period out of the consciousness of a certain quantity of things to be got into it—details, contingencies, cross-references, explanations, analogues—without which his statement might be judged incomplete. Its job is more and more to *contain,* less and less to *discover* and *display.* The element of free inquiry and exploration which gives his earlier writing much of its rare force and expansiveness tends to be replaced by static enumeration, in the process losing for pace and momentum what may have been gained for seriousness of consideration. The danger is not so much of losing direction as simply of overloading. Each sentence still bears an intelligible relation to the governing ends of the whole performance, but this relation is too often *over*elaborated. The consequence is to compound the danger of overloading already present through Melville's commitment to the Romantic virtues of richness of detail and exaggeration of sentiment, and incidentally to dissipate the effects of colloquial freshness and natural variety which his earlier use of first-person narration had confirmed him in.

What especially carries Melville through these dangers in his later work is the continuing seriousness and integrity of his purposes as a writer. His "single-mindedness" (Roy Fuller's phrase, apropos of *The Confidence-Man*) increases, without lessening his extraordinary tactical inventiveness—though there is also an increasing risk of monotony. Unity of apprehension gives him some margin for discontinuity and indirection, in prose syntax as in argument. It is one source, specifically, of that radical exactness of diction in *The Confidence-Man* and *Billy Budd* which continually gives point and emphasis to what would otherwise be a disabling contortion of ordinary statement.

From the first, Melville's sentences are units of definition as well as of expression; this is true even while, as still in *Moby-Dick,* they are preponderantly affective or pictorial. But after *Pierre* their characteristic behavior—what they count for and do as distinct from how they are constructed—noticeably alters. They no longer act *primarily* to thrust upon us the feelings, sensations, material densities, excitements, and felt intimations of the encountered things of "this world." The qualities that sustain *Moby-Dick,* the sensuous charm, the verbal music, the kinetic tension and urgency, seem relatively muted, even withheld, in the later stories. What the more remarkable sentences now appear to respond to are the whole conceived forms of the cycles of action and motive in the matters being presented. Not the intrinsic nature of the things we give names to but their phenomenal cadence and succession, the enacted logic of their known being, now direct Melville's concern and shape his gravest periods. The effort is to put us in contact with some latent rhythm of occurrence at the heart of existence, a rhythm of occurrence governing equally the participation in it and the attempt to know it. The prose that results from this effort is on the whole a serviceable instrument for the directing purposes of Melville's later fiction.

The prose of "Benito Cereno" is symptomatic. Almost nothing in it is detachable from context; it is steadily and admirably subordinated to the peculiar form of the story. As this long narrative-riddle moves tortuously forward to its single violent instant of unraveling, the sentences perform a double function. They must show and they must suspend, both at once; they must communicate tension but also damp it down, though only just so much. The device of very short, nearly discontinuous paragraphing (see above, pages 155–157) makes a contribution here, allowing for rapid shifts and contrasts of accent. But every now and then this taut, constricted prose opens out into something richer and fuller, capable of driving home a major emphasis of no little complexity; and we pass from the bare statement of Captain Delano's impressions to something like the following: "As his foot pressed the half-damp, half-dry sea-mosses matting the place, and a chance phantom cats-paw—an islet of breeze, unheralded, unfollowed—as this ghostly cats-paw came fanning his cheek; as his glance fell upon the row of small, round dead-lights—all closed like coppered eyes of the coffined—and the state-cabin door, once connecting with the gallery, even as the dead-lights had once looked out upon it, but now calked fast like a sarcophagus lid; and to a purple-black, tarred-over panel, threshold, and post; and he bethought him of the time, when that state-cabin and this state-balcony had heard the voices of the Spanish king's officers, and the forms of the Lima viceroy's daughters had perhaps leaned where he stood—as these and other images flitted through his mind, as the cats-paw through the calm, gradually he felt rising a dreamy inquietude, like that of one who alone on the prairie feels unrest from the repose of the noon." The sentence owes much, in carrying through its calculated effort of suspension, to Melville's ordinary descriptive powers, which never ceased to be of a high order. The whole form of it, however, is what I wish to stress here, in particular the rhythm of sensation and response it reproduces; for that rhythm is in miniature the rhythm of the whole action of "Benito Cereno" and correspondingly of its telling.[8]

III

"So paragraphing is a thing that anyone is enjoying. . . ."
—Gertrude Stein, *Narration*

The discipline of paragraphing we mostly take for granted in prose, except when it is missing or when it becomes extraordinarily irregular. The unit of the paragraph is a means, simply, of local organization and arrangement. In prose narrative especially, the pace and rhythm of presentation become as important as the primary naming of materials, and here the manner of paragraphing contributes substantially to the whole form of the composition. The paragraph unit both groups and divides. In neither respect can it afford to appear automatic or perfunctory, a mere function of typography. Rhetorically it operates as the individual sentence operates, though on a broader scale: to place the local materials in the advancing context without smothering their potential suggestiveness, and to control the precise degree of consecutiveness in such a way as

[8] Does not the unusual prevalence, in the sentence, of hyphenated compounds—"half-damp, half-dry sea-mosses," "cats-paw," "state-cabin," "dead-lights," "purple-black, tarred-over"—intensify this effect of suspension?

the dominant logic of the passage (a logic of action, of feeling, of thought, of persuasion) may direct.

A writer like Melville—who thought his way along as he wrote, and was often only roughly aware from one moment to the next of how he meant to carry through his general scheme—is likely to handle the business of paragraphing as he handles everything else in his craft, somewhat opportunistically. He will break off, and project a new start, as often to temper his own distractibleness and reaffirm some displaced emphasis as move ahead to a new one. As Melville's seriousness of intention increased, his practical job as a writer became more and more a matter of striking compromises between the broad narrative conception and the impulse to push every particular intimation through at once to its own speculative ending. The result is the distinctive *periodicity* of his writing. Often as his sentences grow longer and more loaded down, his paragraphs will grow shorter—until in fact the two coalesce in the one-sentence paragraphing characteristic of his later prose. Consider for example the superb first chapter of *The Confidence-Man*. Of fifteen paragraphs, seven consist of a single sentence, more or less elaborate in syntax, while four others contain only two, one of which does nearly all the work. The effect is at once of tightness or involution and yet of a radical casualness of development—an effect that corresponds to the disjointed coherence of the book as a whole.[9]

The same periodistic unwinding of the thread of exposition is evident in *Billy Budd* and makes, I think, a substantial contribution to the remarkable narrative economy of that work. A striking instance occurs in Chapter 13, at the climax of the patiently analytic characterization of Claggart (the last of the three principals to be so presented). The main argument of the chapter ends in a sentence that is a marvel of tact and con-

[9] Paragraphs of one sentence are as frequent in *Typee*, *Omoo*, and *Mardi*, but what they chiefly indicate in those haphazardly assembled books is short-windedness and a *lack* of consistent purpose.

trolled energy, that both denominates and dramatizes. The immediate point is Claggart's reaction to the "moral phenomenon" presented in Billy Budd. Mostly, Melville writes of him, he feels a "cynic disdain—disdain of innocence—to be nothing more than innocent!" "Yet in an aesthetic way he saw the charm of it, the courageous free-and-easy temper of it, and fain would have shared it, but he despaired of it." The immediate force of this is that it confirms in a highly specific précis the whole cumulative history of Claggart's association with Billy. It does so the more effectively by standing at the end of the chapter's long main paragraph; the rhetorical climax is ratified by the typographical division. That division equally affects, of course, what follows. A one-sentence paragraph now concludes the chapter, in a fine summary cadence that gains noticeably by being thus introduced and set apart: "With no power to annul the elemental evil in him, though readily enough he could hide it; apprehending the good, but powerless to be it; a nature like Claggart's surcharged with energy as such natures almost invariably are, what recourse is left to it but to recoil upon itself and like the scorpion for which the Creator alone is responsible, act out to the end the part allotted it."

In Melville's later prose the forms of sentence and paragraph adapt themselves almost too submissively to the pressure of the thought. They give way a little too quickly to its multiplying qualifications. But at each step, in turn, the outward casualness of the construction and the seeming oddness of local emphasis are sustained by the steadiness of argumentative purpose. For the method of exposition Melville had come to favor as a story-teller such tactics served him fairly well. From the first, in the case of *Billy Budd*, the narrative voice holds the action at a remove and works by a kind of filtered and distilled recollection, issuing not so much in any continuous dramatic succession as in a series of vivid tableaux; and for this the periodism of the writing seems peculiarly in keeping, making itself a positive instrument of the narrative's developing statement.[10]

So in general this periodism—if I may be allowed the coinage; I mean to suggest something other than the rhetorical mechanism of periodic syntax—with its running rhythm of suspension, climax, and definition, is the effective means of the thoroughness and deliberation that characterize Melville's best work. Though its tendency is to break the ordinary narrative continuity, the instinct for consolidation and completeness of statement that it promotes will often turn an apparent interruption into an especially effective confirming flourish. There are paragraphs in *Moby-Dick* which we feel are drawn from the author's deepest penetration into his most challenging materials, but which oddly have the appearance—or so it seems as we begin them—of afterthoughts. The spring of the writer's imagination, coiled to its work, now pulses again as if under its own free power; and the mastered shape of the paragraph unit provides it a natural interval to move through. One fine instance of this effect is the paragraph in Chapter 41 (see above, page 110) developing the figure of the Hôtel de Cluny and the Roman ruins beneath it to represent all that must remain undefined in the character of Ahab. Another is the buoyantly Ishmaelian paragraph closing out Chapter 86, "The Tail," in which the tremendous mysteries of the sperm whale's behavior are compared finally with the invisibility, as told in Exodus, of the face of God. The virtuosity of these paragraphs and of others like them results in good part from their simultaneous compactness of form and free assembling of unanticipated further data. Their construction, their very existence in the

[10] A good case of the serviceability of these long and short paragraphs, and the short and long sentences within them, is the charming serio-comic sketch, "I and My Chimney." But in "The Bell-Tower," a rare (for Melville) exercise in the stricter Hawthornesque form of dramatic allegory and (to my taste) one of his few distinct failures, the writing seems cramped and obstructed; we feel for once a serious disparity between the form adopted and the writer's natural mode of elaboration.

text, appearing to some degree accidental, they are that much more able to push the argument ahead without constraint, and then to stop at a point of real strength.

IV

In all Melville's work through *Moby-Dick* the short chapter is the practical basis of the presentation. For the kind of documentary, episodic adventure-chronicle he was writing, it is the main ordering device. It becomes the simple means of piecing out the narrative, of moving easily from one thing to the next or of building quickly but with a sufficient illusion of suspense to some short-run climax. The short chapter nicely suited Melville's raw talent in his first books, a talent principally for spot description and ruminative reporting. It served equally well the subsequent flaring of his ambition and competence as a writer. A unit of discourse is also a unit of conception; and for the eager, opportunistic, quick-opening bursts of Melville's expanding imagination, a better compositional scheme than the loose string of relatively self-contained chapters is hard to think of.

In *Typee* and *Omoo* there is already an attractive, a "magazinish," compactness to each successive chapter. Certain ones —the disquisition on breadfruit in *Typee*, the sketch of the sailor Rope-yarn in *Omoo*—have the simple efficiency of set-pieces; they are neatly turned, but also conscientiously detailed and informative. The risk incurred is fragmentation, and in the overblown structure of *Mardi* this shortness of narrative breath too exactly expresses the diffuseness of the whole. In the better-defined effort of *Redburn* and *White-Jacket*, on the other hand, the unit of the short chapter is felt more positively as an instrument of form, a means of concentrating impressions and themes and of running them through to their short-term limits; in fact, the general line of statement is now shaped to the measure of this unit—or so we think in observing how many chapters in these two lively chronicles rise to a distinct terminal flourish in a manner worthy of *Moby-Dick*.

After *Moby-Dick* individual chapters are less remarkable in themselves, and appear less determinative formally. With *Pierre* the strain of the effort to write "a regular romance, with a mysterious plot to it, & stirring passions at work"—as the author described the book to his English publisher—results in the odd formal compromise of "Books" sub-divided into short numbered sections, an arrangement that does, at least, help to salvage some degree of organization and pace from the chaos of Melville's purposes. Subsequently, in *Israel Potter* and *The Confidence-Man*, and also (not to be overlooked in this reckoning) *Clarel*, the unit of the chapter reappears to do its job of local division and emphasis. But only, perhaps, in *Billy Budd* does it once again play a vital part in the whole creative achievement. The sentence-making in *Billy Budd* gropes somewhat, but the chapters positively race in their succession, their juxtapositions of topics and of accents; and the free appositeness and taut grace of their joining, one to the next, produce no small part—so it seems to me—of the impression of completeness and irreversibility that distinguish that extraordinary work in the telling.[11]

With this as with most other phases of Melville's performance, *Moby-Dick* is the major instance. To look for the fullest development of a Melvillean signature, or indeed to think in general about the manner of his mastery as a writer, is (I find) to bring certain chapters and successions of chapters in *Moby-Dick* forcibly to mind. That is not to deny the book coherence as a whole. It is only to recognize certain facts about it: that its improvised practical structure is episodic and capitulatory, and that it finds its coherence not in the mechanism of its plot or in any other unitary (e.g., allegorical or speculative) scheme of presentation but in a continuous major harmony of apprehension—that is to say, in the sufficient assertion, each time

[11] The fine opening chapters of *Israel Potter* and *The Confidence-Man* might also be mentioned. Simply in their forwarding energy, their power to raise and fix our interest, they show Melville at the top of his form, though in both cases the initial momentum is rather wasted.

anew, of a sufficient imaginative power to embrace, and so continue to create, the multiple connections it advances by. The chapter-episodes do, of course, have the advantage of a simple, stirring, naturally suspended main story; but without their continual re-enactment of that story's manifold conditions we would not be held by it as we are. We do the author of *Moby-Dick* no disservice in remembering the grossness of the common fictional conventions—the melodrama, the mystification, the Gothic coloring and theatrical rant—by which he pieced out his grand conception; and then in considering why the book is not spoiled by them. Certainly the drama of Ahab arouses, excitingly enough, a sympathetic curiosity. Certainly the rendering of it appeals very artfully to our readiness to salve our ignorance of the ultimate reason of things with explanatory parables. But it may be, I think, in individual chapters like "The Ship" or "Brit" or "The Grand Armada," that the quick of our consent is touched most compellingly. There Melville gives us plain and full that "sheer apprehension of the world," in D. H. Lawrence's fine words, which in one way or another particularly exacts from us (as we are capable) "a stillness in the soul, an awe."

Other chapters hardly less impressive might be named—and, properly, placed in context, quoted without abridgment, and delivered aloud in full voice like the eloquent recitatives and arias they function as. Certain ones cast in the book's best vein of genial hyperbole ("The Street," or "Nantucket," or—not everyone's choice—"Stubb's Supper," with its perhaps too easy footing in darky humor) would not go unmentioned; nor would those like "The Sermon," or "Moby Dick" and "The Whiteness of the Whale," or "The Try-Works," that are most frequently appealed to for interpretation of the book as a whole; nor others, such as "The First Lowering" and the three chapters of the chase, in which the long narrative series bursts into its studied climaxes of tumultuous action; nor, finally, certain singularly vivid and moving short chapters as compact and resonant as great lyric poems—"The Albatross," "The Pacific," "The Symphony."

None of these, however, needs special pleading. Each has become a touchstone for appreciation of Melville's art and for explanation of his "meaning." For that reason it may be useful to look instead at one or two less spectacular chapters—chapters of the sort that, if accidentally left out in some reprinting, might not immediately be missed. One such is Chapter 110, "Queequeg in His Coffin." It comes just at the beginning of the final rush toward the meeting with Moby Dick, and shares in the renewal of dramatic excitement already underway. And it starts, efficiently, from an incident of some importance to the main action—Ahab's prudential yielding to Starbuck's request to heave to and investigate a leakage of oil in the hold. At once we are deep in technical detail—"tierces," "butts," "casks," "puncheons," "shooks of staves" and "iron bundles of hoops"—and just as quickly this objective data opens out into metaphor; the now topheavy *Pequod* herself bobs "like an air-freighted demijohn," or like "a dinnerless student with all Aristotle in his head." All this is by way of introduction to the main episode of the chapter, which is Queequeg's strange illness and stranger recovery. (I must leave to the reader's own observation the tact with which the chapter's transitions and enlargements are executed.) Typically this episode is launched in a one-sentence paragraph. And that in turn, also typically, opens with an irregular cadence which in its slight artificiality delicately points up the overform of the telling; for in the borrowing of an accent from the style of legend, or of Scripture, the way is prepared for the fable-rounded interlude, the story-within-the-story, which the main narrative pauses here to present: "Now, at this time it was that my poor pagan companion, and fast bosom-friend, Queequeg, was seized with a fever, which brought him nigh to his endless end." The episode now moves along rapidly, but does not pass up its chances for underscoring. So Queequeg's falling ill after his sweated labor deep in the hold permits references, in quick succession, to the seagoing democracy of danger and job-responsibility, to the concrete severities of the ordinary chores of whaling, to the mysteries of body and soul in their joint course through life, and to all the further mysteries of life and death and of everything which, being "truly wondrous and fearful in man, never yet was put into words or books." Queequeg, wasting away into a strange, soft mildness, orders a boat-like coffin made in preparation for certain legendary pagan rites of death; he lies in it, with harpoons, idol-god, and provisions for the last journey; Pip and Starbuck gather to comment, each according to his lights; but then Queequeg, as if by his own "sovereign will and pleasure," decides that it is not really time to die yet, and promptly rallies—and upon his recovery sets about carving certain mystical hieroglyphs upon the coffin (now his sea-chest) which he himself cannot understand. So the chapter ends, but with a last emphasis—Ahab studying these hieroglyphs and crying out in anguish at the tantalizing mystery of them—which not only confirms the obvious correspondences between Queequeg's travail here and Ahab's in the main story but propels us violently back into that story; it is the momentous chapter, "The Pacific," that now follows.

My other example of Melville's ordinary chapter-making in *Moby-Dick*, Chapter 57, has no part at all in the main action. Its title suggests its place in the book, and also the problem of composition it presents: "Of Whales in Paint; in Teeth; in Wood; in Sheet-Iron; in Stone; in Mountains; in Stars." The last chapter in a group of three dealing with pictorial representations and images of the whale, it has the look of a repository for data that will not fit in anywhere else. The semicolons of the title almost flaunt its casualness. But in just this respect it puts us in mind of Melville's most general problems of organization in *Moby-Dick*, for it exemplifies the kind of itemizing of random materials that the whole central mass of the book advances by and that without a determined exertion of imaginative control would have stalled it entirely. There is some point in noting, therefore, that the actual life and charm of this chapter derive in good part from the more than usually emphatic assertion of the narrator's own interposed presence. The chapter is of negligible importance in the over-all design of *Moby-Dick;* nevertheless the same voice speaks in it as in the book's most intensely compelling passages, and speaks as boldly. A mere survey of instances—a painting, the art of skrimshander, savage carvings, roadside emblems, geological formations, the *trompe d'oeil* of natural shapes—rapidly takes on both the thick topicality and the spaciousness of the whole. So in a brief space there is easy reference to Tower-Hill and Wapping, and to all Christendom; one hears of what can be observed "throughout the Pacific, and also in Nantucket, and New Bedford, and Sag Harbor"; a complex panorama of human types and conditions—Iroquois Indians, Hawaiian islanders, cannibals, Greek Achilles and Dutch Dürer, whaling forecastles and gable-roofed houses—is spread out, and succeeded by a complementary panorama of the whole physical earth, revealing fantastic rock-masses under grassy slopes, "amphitheatrical heights" of mountain, and remote and unknown island chains; until finally, "expandingly lifted by your subject," you discover that the tallying of this data has become one with the naming of stars and constellations—Cetus and Argo Navis and the Flying Fish—and so has merged into the mythological origins of all narrative and all experience. The ending (in yet another one-sentence paragraph) is precisely in keeping: "With a frigate's anchors for my bridle-bitts and fasces of harpoons for spurs, would I could mount that whale and leap the topmost skies, to see whether the fabled heavens with all their countless tents really lie encamped beyond my mortal sight." The mythical role Ishmael is roughly cast in being that of the free, versatile, curious, observant, adaptable, irrepressible, democratic everyman at home in all times, places, and conditions—the man born, in the words of the nineteenth-century song, "a hundred thousand years ago," whose report of all he has seen, and not seen, always shows him to be supremely the man upon whom nothing really discoverable has been lost—one cannot think of a fitter epitaph for him (of the kind he sympathetically devises for Bulkington) than this casually magnificent little chapter.

CHAPTER EIGHT

"CERTAIN PHENOMENAL MEN": THE EXAMPLE OF BILLY BUDD

"Ah, who can say what passes between people in such a relation?"—HENRY JAMES, *The Golden Bowl*

IN THE CASE OF *Billy Budd* it may be well to ask at the start just what kind of performance we are dealing with. First of all, it is a narrated story—whatever else we may say of it must take account of the particular manner of its telling. More precisely, it is, in Melville's own phrase, "an inside narrative"; we are to take it as decisively identifying the characters and events it describes, so far as this may ever be done.[1] It is of course an extraordinarily poignant narrative, and one which many readers have felt to be extraordinarily meaningful. The difficulty, to judge from what has been written about it, comes in trying to say what exactly does happen in it and what the meaning is. A great deal of Melville's work, early and late, seems often to have an unsettling effect on the judgments of his readers, not least the more responsive and sympathetic among them. His writing has proved perilously attractive to certain extravagant fashions in present-day criticism, especially that of appealing to a few chosen works of literature for moral

[1] It is possible to read philosophical implications into this phrase, which Melville inscribed in his revised manuscript, in order to support certain ways of interpreting the story as a whole. My own view is simply that in calling his work an "inside narrative," Melville meant only to distinguish it from the kind of false report given in the official *News from the Mediterranean* (Chapter 30), which is all that the world usually knows of such affairs. The events to be related are set down as by one privy to the actual facts of the case, and the narrative is to be valued as a true account.

or even religious authority; or of imputing systems of meaning such as could not practicably be secured within the actual form and scope of the work in question. The warping that results is not unnatural and may indeed express an unusual generosity of response; we all are drawn, in the flush of our involvement with some deeply stirring experience, to see it as containing some conclusive message or as delivering some consummate revelation of our own earnest desiring. No claim of immunity in this respect is made for the present account, which can only take its chances with the rest—and which I offer here in corroboration of the general views of Melville's accomplishment so far advanced.

The ground common to most discussion of *Billy Budd* is the assumption that the story is allegorical—a narrative representation of some universal truth or law or balance of contraries, a parable of Good and Evil, a re-enactment of the Fall, a projected myth of a ritual killing which is also a resurrection, and so on. Such interpretations do not have to be scrambled for. The evidence they adduce is undeniably there. The trouble is rather that the statement of them will seem to miss what one feels, as one reads and re-reads, to be the governing concentration and emphasis of the actual telling. *Billy Budd* is indeed full of quickening intimations as to the larger, the perhaps universal circumstance of human life—intimations which are typical of Melville's imagination, as his explicitness in articulating them is typical of his best performance as a writer. But the decisive narrative logic and cogency of the story are, I think, to be found elsewhere. They are to be found in an effort which Melville characteristically troubled to furnish precise words for, the effort to "define and denominate certain phenomenal men" (Chapter 11). To render in force and detail through all the incident and commentary of his narrative the essential feature and bearing of these men, to name and make authoritative the example of character manifested in them—this is what seems to me to lie at the heart of Melville's enterprise. In *Billy Budd* he undertakes to define not universal truth but certain specific and contingent examples of being and behavior.

This undertaking is not to be felt in equal force at every point in the story. In the opening chapters a reader looking into *Billy Budd* for the first time, without benefit of editorial introductions but with some knowledge of Melville's earlier books, would be very likely to suppose that he had come upon another *Israel Potter*. Melville (as a study of his manuscript changes makes evident) had his difficulties in determining the best use of his materials and in discovering the proper drift and consequence of his story. In some respects his problem, though on a different scale, resembles that of Hardy a few years later in *The Dynasts:* both works, looking back a century to the strange apocalyptic wars of a long-vanished time, are not unconcerned with the particular ideological issues of that time; yet both mean to place the ultimate causes and meaning of the events recorded in the working of less contingent forces. So *Billy Budd* opens with several chapters on the historical background—the war with revolutionary France, the naval mutinies—and repeatedly turns aside to show how this bears upon the action. In fact, Melville goes further and introduces or intimates what might seem to be even more restrictive considerations, aligning Captain Vere (and himself as narrator) with a philosophic anti-Jacobinism, calling one ship the *Rights-of-Man* and another the *Athéiste,* and so forth. All this is clearly meant to inform the story. But it is not meant to explain the story. The historical circumstances touch on the story at every crisis but do not essentially determine it. We are to feel both elements, the framing conditions and the special action, as real and consequential; the era intensifies our sense of the event as the event substantiates our impression of the era; but each is to be apprehended as following its own logic. The trouble is that if we respond at all to the impressive terms and symbols Melville used to embody his story, we may press upon them too rigid or predetermined an arrangement; we may be misled (as E. M. Forster cautioned with regard to *Moby-Dick*) "into harmonizing the incidents" and so screen out the distinguishing "roughness and richness" of the narrative as a whole.[2]

II

I do not mean to dismiss out of hand the various allegorical interpretations of *Billy Budd.* If only in their striking variety and equal conviction, they have much to tell us—about the nature of Melville's writing as well as about the excitements and hazards of criticism. No one has worked along this line of approach more discerningly than Professor Norman Holmes Pearson, whose findings have the merit of standing near the center of sensible opinion on the story and may serve briefly —I hope not unfairly—as a stalking horse.[3] To Professor Pearson, *Billy Budd* is best understood by analogy to Milton's heroic poems: "What Melville was doing was to try to give in as universalized a way as possible . . . another redaction of the myth which had concerned Milton . . . in the trilogy of his three major works"—the Christian myth, that is, of the fall from innocence and the promise of redemption.

There are of course numerous particulars to support such an interpretation, and Professor Pearson and others have mustered them cogently; they need not be reviewed here. What does need to be said is commonplace enough: that the analogies Melville brings forward in support of his story—Billy as Adam, his hanging as a kind of Ascension, the yardarm as the True Cross, and so on—prove nothing in themselves about either his intention or his achievement. This is not simply because

[2] *Aspects of the Novel* (New York, 1927), p. 200.

[3] "*Billy Budd:* 'The King's Yarn,'" *American Quarterly,* III (Summer 1951), 99–114.

Justification for the diversity of critical comment *Billy Budd* has given rise to is suggested by the penetrating judgment of the poet Montale, that the story is at one and the same time an epic, a tale of adventure, a Platonic dialogue, a critical essay, and a mystery play: "An Introduction to *Billy Budd*" (1942), *Sewanee Review,* LXVII (Summer 1960), 419–422.

they are matched by an equal number of analogies of a quite different sort (so Billy, for example, is also compared to Apollo, to Hercules, to a Tahitian of Captain Cook's time courteously but indifferently receiving the ministrations of Christian missionaries, and to a St. Bernard dog). We are also to bear in mind that we are reading a nineteenth-century, not a seventeenth-century, writer; in Melville's time the literary apprehension of Christian myth was nearly as divorced from sacramental religion, and as merely moral and pathetic when not wholly sentimental, as the apprehension of classical myth. But in any case we need above all to look to the whole development of Melville's actual narrative and to the particular disposition and intensity of its insistences. The question is: how do all these evidences operate in the story? do they determine the action and constitute its first meaning? or are they at most a kind of illustrative commentary, suggesting by familiar analogy the appropriate pitch of feeling?

There is little doubt that Melville meant his story to be in some manner exemplary and that as he worked on it he found it profoundly moving; he "believed" in it. The strength of intimation in an inveterate explainer like Melville is in some proportion to the weight and spur of his own perplexities. The religious metaphors in *Billy Budd* do indeed confirm our sense of a religious depth in Melville's sensibility. But we must be wary of abstracting the stuff of these metaphors from his immediate deployment of them—the obvious temptation, but somehow especially insidious with this work. Melville himself is explicit about his procedures. Reaching the limit of observation and analysis in his presentation of John Claggart, he turns for a clinching notation to the Scriptural formula of the "mysteries of iniquity" (Chapter 12). Now what he was trying to express seems to me sufficiently identified in that precisely climactic phrase, which perfectly secures his idea of the "something defective and abnormal" in the constitution of the master-at-arms. But Melville himself recognized and characteristically specified the risk he was taking in thus falling back, here and elsewhere, on the "lexicon of Holy Writ" in an age which had grown indifferent to it, which could no longer be relied on to understand all that might be involved in it. His caution is itself pointedly cautionary. For our time is not so much skeptical of religious doctrines and symbols—certainly not passionately and burdensomely skeptical as Melville was—as it is ignorant of them, which Melville was not. Perhaps the first truth about us in this respect is that we are the embarrassed receivers of (in Carlo Levi's phrase) a civilization which used to be Christian. We respect, we are in a civil way habituated to, the positions of Christian belief; but the norms of our experience no longer reinforce them. And finding in a document like *Billy Budd* that this half-forgotten vocabulary has been restored to use, we may be overimpressed, mistaking mere unembarrassed familiarity with it for a reconstitution of its prime significance. But to make of *Billy Budd* an attempt, and an attempt comparable to Milton's, to reanimate the Christian myth of human destiny under divine law is to respond less to the limiting and authenticating particulars of Melville's story than to the pathos of its corroborative analogies and allusions, or perhaps to the transferred pathos of our own progressive disregard of them. Also it is to claim for Melville the kind of positive testament or settled belief which seems inconsistent with what we know of him; which all his tenacity in doubt, his frank and courageous ignorance, his respect for the discomforts of truth and the phenomenal ambiguities of existence, would have gone to keep him from taking refuge in, even for the space of a story, even at the end of his life.

No, the actual telling of *Billy Budd* will not bear so grand a burden of meaning, and was not intended to. What its limiting circumstances are, Melville is concerned to say as precisely as he can. His use of the military setting in constraint of the events of his story is to the point here. The martial law by which Billy goes to his death is usually held to be symbolic of some universal law or authority, such as divine providence: I think mistakenly. Nor can I follow Professor Richard Chase in comparing it with the "abstract legality" confronted by Antigone or the "inhumanly enforced legality" of *The Winter's Tale;* for the official agencies of justice in these plays are to be understood as wrong precisely in that, being "abstract" and "inhuman," they are other than what they ought to be. But Melville is at some pains to present the martial law as morally *sui generis,* and in its own terms morally unimpeachable. It is designed, he reminds us, solely to subserve the extraordinary circumstance of war. It is "War's child," as Captain Vere tells the court, and must of its nature look "but to the frontage, the appearance" of things—and not wrongly. As against moral or divine law it can have no regard to questions of motive or judgments of virtue: "The prisoner's deed—with that alone we have to do." It is for this terrible eventuality alone, otherwise it would be indefensible. But in the circumstances Melville sets out, there is no appeal from it.

Why Melville's story rides so easily in this rigid context, and what it gains from it, are absorbing questions, but beyond the compass of the present essay.[4] My point now is simply that in

[4] The search for answers might begin with Vigny's *Servitudes et Grandeurs Militaires* (1835), which provides, I think, a much truer parallel to *Billy Budd* than Milton's majestic poems. The resemblances are striking. Both Vigny and Melville (each having elsewhere, in *Stello* and *Pierre,* dramatized the Romantic theme of the suffering and heroism of the creative imagination) discovered in the action of obedience to martial discipline a more compelling occasion for moral drama; both responded to the resignation and self-effacement of military service as a more profoundly moving symbol of imaginable virtue. Indeed Vigny's notation of "a certain puerility" in the military character sheds light on a controversial aspect of the character of Billy Budd—as his treatment of Collingwood, in which we are asked specifically to apprehend "all that the sense of duty can subdue in a great soul," sheds light on Captain Vere. (Melville, we may note, had also paid his respects to Collingwood, and for the same reasons, in *White-Jacket.*)

Curiously it is Vigny's book which is the more didactic, being openly concerned to advance a general moral discipline for a post-Christian culture. "Is anything still sacred?" Vigny asked: "in the universal foundering of creeds, to what wreckage can brave hands still cleave?" His answer was that "creeds are weak, but man is strong," and he went on in his closing

Billy Budd martial law and the "military necessity" are accepted in their own right, without ulterior design. Melville does not choose, as he did in *White-Jacket,* to judge the martial discipline by a higher moral law; he makes such a standard available neither to Vere and the court in their search for the right action (though they reach out to it) nor to the reader in judging what has happened. Christian conscience, mercy, the judgment of God—these are neither directly opposed to martial law nor put aside as meaningless. Melville has Vere speak of such considerations as having the force of "Nature" in the hearts of men but as being, in the "singular" given case, inapplicable. Doctrines of Christianity are invoked in full support of the pathos of the story, but assent to them is not what is at stake. It interested Melville, indeed it profoundly moved him, to point out in passing how one part of his narrative seemed to confirm the Calvinist doctrine of depravity or how another suggested the "heresy" of natural innocence, but these propositions are not, as such, his subject or argument. The whole movement of suggestion in Melville's narrative seems to me the reverse of allegorical; the words and names for the action of the story, the thoughts and analogies that help define it, follow from it and are subject to it. The image of the action itself, of a particular occurrence involving particular persons, stands first.

In *Billy Budd* this image is constituted first of all by the three main characters, and the action proceeds from the capacity of spirit painstakingly attributed to each of them. Each is set before us as a kind of natural force; in fact Melville's probing curiosity projects what might seem a thoroughly deterministic explanation of their behavior if it was not so clearly

---

chapter to describe a "religion of Honor," which is characterized by "manly decency" and the "passive grandeur" of personal abnegation: "Whereas all other virtues seem to be sent down from Heaven to take us by the hand and raise us up, this alone appears to be innate and to be straining heavenwards. It is a wholly human virtue, born of the earth and earning no heavenly reward after death. It is indeed the virtue of the life of this world." The implicit logic of Melville's rendering of his two heroes could not be stated more sympathetically.

in the service of a stubborn and wondering sense of their free agency. "Character" is in general rather curiously exhibited here, Melville's language repeatedly suggesting that it is best apprehended at any given moment by a kind of *savoring*. A man's character derives from the accumulated conditions (the seasonings, so to speak) of his whole life, and so registers as a "taste" or "flavor" on the "moral palate," as though too subtly compounded for stricter definition. It may be that no sequence of dramatic events will wholly communicate this distinguishing savor of character; the necessities of action, in art as in life, show little enough respect for persons. But the mode of exposition Melville turned to has other resources than dramatization, other ways of declaring its meanings. So the climax of this minutely specifying narration is reached in an episode in which the actual event is withheld, and we are referred instead to the *character* of the participants.

This is the episode in which, the trial over, Vere privately tells Billy the court's decision. Given in very nearly the shortest chapter of the narrative (Chapter 23), it follows the longest and most detailed; and in contrast to the thorough exposition just concluded (of Vere's distress, the hesitant proceedings of the court, the ambiguities of the evidence, and all Vere's patient argument) it moves instead by conjecture and reticence. "Beyond the communication of the sentence," the main section of it begins, "what took place at this interview was never known." Yet on this elliptical passage the full weight of the narrative, accelerating after its slow-paced beginnings into the drama of the middle chapters, centers and falls, its steady simple movement coming full stop. By working so sensible a change of pace and manner, and by explicitly likening the hidden event to what must happen wherever in the world the circumstances are "at all akin to those here attempted to be set forth," Melville appears for the moment to be concentrating our attention on the very heart of his whole conception. What we are told is what it chiefly concerns him to have us know—

the phenomenal quality of character in his two heroes. In their essential being Vere and Billy are as one, "each radically sharing in the rarer qualities of our nature—so rare indeed as to be all but incredible to average minds however much cultivated." On this basis and in these limited terms the narrator will risk "some conjectures." But insofar as his conjecture does accord with the rarity of spirit by which he has identified his protagonists, it may lead into the profoundest truth, it may be definitive.

So the chapter's central paragraph begins: "It would have been in consonance with the spirit of Captain Vere. . . ." The capacity of spirit being known, the weight and bearing of the event may be measured and its meaning grasped. And what capacity of spirit Melville meant to set before us begins to be confirmed in the virtues he gravely imagines as "not improbably" brought into play in the interview: in Vere, utter frankness and unselfishness, making him confess his own part in Billy's sentencing, and intensifying into the compassion of a father; in Billy an equal frankness, and bravery of course, but also joy, in the realization of his Captain's extraordinary trust. Yet these impressive virtues are in a way incidental. What draws the narrator on is the magnitude of the capability they speak for. Translated out of their customary stations, Vere and Billy meet as "two of great Nature's nobler order." Their entire competence of spirit before the event is assumed; only the immediate exercise of it goes past saying. Though the narration here makes a show of drawing back even from conjecture, the quality and the significance of the action continue to be defined; exact terms are used. Melville writes that "there is no telling the sacrament" when two such spirits embrace, but the very word "sacrament" precisely advances his explanation. The same tactic directs the closing sentence of this astonishing paragraph: "There is privacy at the time, inviolable to the survivor, and holy oblivion, the sequel to each diviner magnanimity, providentially covers all at last." Here again the withholding is according to the inmost nature of that which is being disclosed; the "privacy" of the scene is a consequence of the great and rare virtue, the "magnanimity," at work in it.[5]

May we not take this explanation, and the word that thus concludes it, as literally as we can? As with martial law, Melville's purpose was not to universalize the particular phenomenon, the capacity of spirit generating this encounter, but simply to identify it, to declare it in its own name. In Vere and Billy, the passage affirms, we have to do with magnanimity, with greatness of soul, a quality which, though "all but incredible to average minds however much cultivated," is nevertheless according to nature, and is touched with divinity—or whatever in human conduct is suggestive of divinity. Though it is constrained by Claggart's depravity of spirit (also "according to nature") and has still to undergo the pitiless operation of the "military necessity," this greatness of soul in the two heroes achieves in the sacrament of their coming together an "inviolable," a "diviner" magnanimity. As there is a mystery of iniquity in Claggart, there is a mystery of magnanimity in these two. It is given no power to prevent the now settled outcome of the

[5] This view of what Melville was driving at in *Billy Budd,* and of his deliberateness in getting to it, is reinforced by examination of the manuscript drafts of this passage (in the Houghton Library, at Harvard). In its first form the paragraph is somewhat differently phrased; Vere and Billy are called simply "two of the nobler order," and the passage ends: "and holy oblivion the desirable thing for each diviner magnanimity, naturally ensues." Rewriting—his corrections are pencilled in—Melville brought into sharper focus the suggestion of "naturally" by crossing out the adverb itself but then enlarging the preceding phrase to "two of great Nature's nobler order." This allowed him to introduce a further perspective with "providentially," as if to call to mind that wider frame of being within which not only the life of man but the encompassing life of all creation is circumscribed. The change in the last clause corresponds. In speaking of what would be the "desirable thing," Melville had rounded off his idea too restrictively; with the apparently neutral word "sequel" he reached out past subjective wish to an indifferent order of nature and providence which to his imagination all human actions belong to and gain dignity from, and which an event so charged as this with emotion and with necessity would most vividly exemplify.

What he did not change is also significant. In both versions, it will be noticed, the center of gravity in the closing sentence is the same: "each diviner magnanimity."

action. Yet its radiance is beyond catastrophe. It is such as can survive those decisive accidents of individual existence—age, health, station, luck, particular experience—which Melville consistently presented the lives of his characters as being determined by. Now the narrative has come to its defining climax. Here the tone is set for what remains to be told, and not at the pitch of tragedy—the tone of exalted acceptance and muted patient joy which will be heard in the account of Billy in irons like a "slumbering child," in Billy's "God bless Captain Vere!" in Vere's dying with Billy's name on his lips (not in remorse, Melville specifies), and finally, and with what sure art, in the gravely acquiescent music of the closing ballad.

III

This view of the action of *Billy Budd* (a view not discouraged by the dedication to the "great heart" of Jack Chase) does not, I think, deny the story any power of suggestion or degree of achievement. Perhaps it may remove the sense of disproportion between theme and occasion which Professor Pearson's and kindred readings leave us with, yet at the same time increase the interest of Melville's actual accomplishment. For an idea of some fulfilled greatness of soul lies, as we know, at the center not only of classical tradition in moral philosophy and literature but of Christian tradition as well. It lies also (as securely as ideas of equality and civil liberty) at the heart of the democratic ethos. The great-souled man—what significant reckoning of our duty and destiny, whether in the mode of tragedy or satire or prophecy or simple witness, does not somehow take account of him? For what else do we especially revere a Washington and a Lincoln, whose unique place in the national pantheon is surely something more than the sum of their historical deeds? And what more momentous question can be put to the democratic writer than the question of greatness of mind and spirit in a mass society?

To follow out this view of the story might well lead into discussion of Melville's "Americanism," an absorbing matter certainly, though at present rather shopworn. Just as usefully it may lead us back to a parallel which I have made some point here of questioning—the example of Milton. The Milton who matters here, however, is not the Christian poet of paradise lost and regained but the prideful humanist whose dedication to the idea of magnanimity is proverbial in English letters. Milton's concern with this virtue in his writings, and his explicit pride in the pursuit of it in his life, are in fact foremost among the qualities which have given him his peculiar personal aura and earned him so much gratuitous personal hostility in our own anti-heroic times. They are also of the essence of his Protestantism, and it is not likely to be altogether accidental that the two writers of epic imagination and enterprise in the Protestant camp (if we may imagine one) of Anglo-American literature should show a common concern, a considered preoccupation, with magnanimity.

As we might expect, Milton was confident and unembarrassed in deploying the term. He used it consistently and (according to his lights) precisely, to denote a summary condition of virtuousness in which the lesser particular virtues were gathered up and lifted to grandeur; in this he followed the Aristotelian definition of magnanimity as the "crowning ornament" of the virtuous character (*Nich. Ethics,* IV, iii, 16). What is especially Miltonic is his emphasis on rational self-consciousness in the exercise of magnanimity. For him the concept signifies the highest reach of that "pious and just honoring of ourselves" which is a duty of the virtuous man second only to love of God. Cultivation of magnanimity thus becomes the great end of education—so we find him saying in this famous and characteristic sentence: "I call therefore a compleat and generous Education that which fits a man to perform justly, skillfully, and magnanimously all the offices both private and public of Peace and War." But to describe the ideal education is to consider what end man was born for; and it is in the account of the creation of Adam that we come to the furthest reach of Milton's idea:

> There wanted yet the Master work, the end
> Of all yet don; a Creature who not prone
> And Brute as other Creatures, but endu'd
> With Sanctitie of Reason might erect
> His Stature, and upright with Front serene
> Govern the rest, self-knowing, and from thence
> Magnanimous to correspond with Heav'n. . . .

In magnanimity, so conceived, natural creation rises to its sovereign beauty and fulfillment. Would any nineteenth-century transcendentalist or mystical democrat ever claim more than this for the instructed soul of man?

Of these associations some were still viable for Melville but not all. It was precisely a doctrinal confidence in what the great-souled man might "correspond with" that, two hundred years later, his intelligence despaired of. At the same time certain outwardly passive virtues like humility and disinterestedness had come to seem far more positive and potentially heroic than they had been to Milton in his time. So Melville could specify in Vere a "certain unaffected modesty of manhood" without diminishing his general "ascendancy of character" or his Miltonic readiness for all private and public offices of peace and war. It is still, however, a traditionally heroic image of magnanimity that we are shown at the beginning of *Billy Budd* in the chapters on Nelson. Nelson's greatness in command is assumed; what concerned Melville was his personal behavior at Trafalgar and the charge of "vainglory" and "affectation" it lay open to. And though Melville was on the defensive here, he unequivocally championed the impulse of the great-hearted hero to display his greatness and love the glory of it. Given "a nature like Nelson" and the opportunity of a Trafalgar, then the "sort of priestly motive" that directed the great commander's conduct was, Melville insisted in one of his showiest sentences, altogether natural and fitting, coming from that "exaltation of sentiment" which is the mark of the truly heroic action.[6]

The point is not that Milton's conception of magnanimity is a "source" of *Billy Budd*. What we are considering is not a case of "influence" but a comparable turn and reach of mind, formed in a broadly common moral tradition though expressing very different stages in its devolution. To Milton magnanimity was within the achieving of every wise and good man, a condition of completed moral being to be reached through rational procedures of education and piety. To Melville it was a rarer thing —much less a condition to be achieved, much more a mysterious distillation of certain transactions and contingencies in certain men's lives. At the high tide of his creative energy he could imagine it as naturally resulting from that "unshackled, democratic spirit of Christianity" in which America seemed destined to lead the world; we know how quickly this confidence went out of him. He found himself unable to assume even a moral efficacy in magnanimity, since he could not be sure in the first place of the moral order of creation, any more than he could have much faith in the moral justness of American society; both seemed paralyzingly indifferent to degrees of virtue. Nor could he take refuge in ideas of the infinitude of the private man or of the priesthood of the individual soul, as the simpler Protestant and democratic optimisms of his time would encourage him to. This being so, his undertaking in *Billy Budd*, and his success in it, are all the more impressive.

But did he in fact succeed? The character and role of Captain Vere fit well enough the traditional notion of magnanimity, but what about the character of Billy Budd? What has Miltonic

[6] This defense of Nelson's love of glory, it may be noted, fits perfectly the Aristotelian concept of greatness of soul, according to which, "honor is the object with which the great-souled are concerned, since it is honor above all else which great men claim and deserve." Furthermore, "he that claims less than he deserves is small-souled. . . ." *Nich. Ethics*, IV, iii, 8 and 11.

magnanimity to do with the "mindless innocence" (as Professor Chase has put it) of the boy sailor? Given the character Melville presents, how much can be claimed for it? "To be nothing more than innocent!"—Claggart's "cynic disdain" may not be unreasonable; in one form or another it has been shared by most critics of the story. Have we not, in Billy, an expression of sentiment poignant in itself but unassimilated and unresolved in the narrative, and best explained (as Professor Chase would explain it) by the life-history and personal necessities of the author? [7]

But magnanimity, we may note again, is not a substantive virtue. No particular actions prove it or follow from it. What the word describes is a certain dimension of spirit which the virtuous man may rise to and which any moral event may conceivably participate in. Whatever has a soul (and to Melville's excruciating animism anything can seem to) may in certain extraordinary circumstances grow into the condition of magnanimity, the soul that is called innocent not less than the soul instructed by experience. If innocence is compatible with virtuousness—and in characterizing Billy, Melville did not doubt that it is: "a virtue went out of him"—then it too is capable of its own kind of magnanimity.

Here again we may appeal to Melville's care to be explicit; for in working out his conception of the character of Billy Budd —a "child-man" not incapable of moral reflection yet mysteriously uncorrupted, able to conceive of death but like a savage warrior "wholly without irrational fear of it"—Melville does in fact "denominate" it categorically. This is in a passage of explanation added to Chapter 16 of the revised draft, just after Billy has been approached by an apparent conspiracy of mutiny (though in his innocence he has hardly understood it as that). Melville, first specifying that the thought of reporting these overtures never entered Billy's mind, pushes on to a

[7] Richard Chase, "Introduction," *Selected Tales and Poems by Herman Melville* (New York, 1950), pp. xiii–xvi.

more positive claim, though at the moment a superfluous one: even if the step of reporting what he had heard *had* been suggested to him, "he would have been deterred from taking it by the thought, one of novice-magnanimity, that it would savor overmuch of the dirty work of a tell-tale." A special sort of magnanimity, awkwardly qualified and, though capable of choosing between evils, not yet decisively tested: nevertheless Melville makes it the defining motive in his conjecture here. Notice, too, that the term is introduced to attribute to Billy a natural revulsion from the role of informer; for in this he is sensibly at one with Captain Vere, who will respond to Claggart's accusations in the same way. To the magnanimous man, conscious of his nature and of the reputation it rightfully deserves, there may be a greater sin than breach of the ninth commandment but there is none more loathsome. It is a sudden intuition that Claggart is bearing false witness which goads Vere into the intemperate threat of the yard-arm-end, and so gives the master-at-arms his right to a full hearing; it is "horror" of his accuser, as against mere "amazement" at the accusation, that paralyzes Billy in Claggart's presence.

Can Melville's intention be doubted: to show Vere and Billy as bound to one another in a complementary greatness of soul?[8] As the story moves on to the music of its close we are shown how each in his own way has instructed the other; how, so to speak, the magnanimity possible to virtuous innocence has fulfilled itself and in turn given its mysterious blessing to the

[8] The question of Billy's moral nature, and its progress through the story, may need a few words more. At several points in the narrative Melville takes time to describe the exact blend of character in Billy as it affects the action then going forward; each time he shows Billy occupied in positive moral considerations (Chapters 17, 22, 25). In Chapters 25 and 26 it is suggested that Billy has undergone a degree of visible (or only just not invisible) change as a result of his "tension of agony." His "rare personal beauty" is "spiritualized," the skull begins "delicately to be defined" beneath the skin. But these suggestions are muted and unforced. An allegorical demonstration of the progress of the soul does not seem intended. By way of contrast, think how Hawthorne might have handled this action; did handle it, in fact, in *The Marble Faun*.

world-sustaining magnanimity of experienced and commissioned virtue. The first represents that part of man which, being born to nature, remains of nature; the second represents that part of man which is uniquely of his own making, his defining burden as a moral and historical creature. Melville is explicit about what has happened. The "tension of agony" in Billy, he wrote, "survived not the something healing in the closeted interview with Captain Vere"; in turn Billy, restored to the role of "peacemaker," has lifted Vere, for all his anguish, beyond remorse. The motions of magnanimity under the most agonizing worldly duress: that is Melville's image and his theme.

By way of elaboration, we have been shown three fulfillments of human nature—on one side depravity (or "monomania," his word for Claggart as for Ahab), on the other these two forms of magnanimity self-realized through recognition of one another. No exact balance is struck. We sense some division of intention or disequilibrium. Midway in the story, for example, it is the conflict between the two sides that engrosses interest, or the attack of the one upon the other. But in the showdown Claggart is not allowed to be any real match for the other two,[9] and we see that Melville's most profound intention lies further along. It is seldom observed how pitiable Claggart is, in a way in which Billy and Vere are not. Once acting in the open he cannot really deceive the Captain or leave any lasting scar on Billy—though his own understrappers deceive him at will (Chapter 14), as indeed he deceives himself; it is not usually pointed out that Claggart believes his absurd accusation. He is envious and despairing, an embodiment of those life-denying "sins refined" which in *Clarel* were Melville's vision of Sodom and Gomorrah. But he is not a hypocrite (as was Bland, the master-at-arms of *White-Jacket*). In such a nature, Melville made a point of explaining, conscience functions not in restraint

[9] Another of Melville's revisions is worth noting in this respect. Describing Claggart's response to "the moral phenomenon presented in Billy Budd" (Chapter 13), he struck out this too schematic remark: "In him he recognized his own direct opposite. . . ."

of its terrible determinations but as their helpless agent. Also it is not usually observed how abruptly and entirely Claggart and what is embodied in him are dismissed from the story. After the trial he is barely mentioned again; no trace of his concerted malignity is allowed to survive the interview between Vere and Billy. It is as though Melville's conception of the radically opposing crystallizations possible to human nature—confidence and envy, love and hate, frankness and dissimulation, assurance and despair, magnanimity and depravity—had swung clear of his tormenting search for belief, so that he was free to rise at the climax of his story to a different and surer theme: the conjunction of the two magnanimities, making sacrifice to the military necessity.

IV

"The only great ones among mankind are the poet, the priest, and the soldier; the man who sings, the man who blesses, and the man who sacrifices, and sacrifices himself." It is not, I think, the grand design of Christian myth nor the example of Greek tragedy or Miltonic epic but this confessional aphorism of Baudelaire's that stands nearest the logic and authority of *Billy Budd.*[10] Strong judgments of life-in-general, of good and evil and law and justice, may throb through Melville's narrative, but its work is not to prove them. It asks not, "what is life?" or "what are the ways of God?" or even "what is justice?" but, "given this imaginable event in these circumstances, what power of response is there in certain phenomenal men?" So we are shown one kind of greatness of spirit in Vere, the soldier-priest of the military necessity, joining with another kind in Billy Budd, whose power to bless transfigures not only his own life. We observe, as in Baudelaire's journal or Vigny's *Servitudes et Grandeurs Militaires,* how an apprehension of the moral chaos and inscrutability of the experienced world has been held in balance by an austere intuition of honor and of

[10] *Mon Coeur Mis à Nu,* No. 48.

personal abnegation. Yet for all their poignancy the specific terms of Melville's narrative do not require our option. Far less than in *Moby-Dick* or *Pierre* or *The Confidence-Man* or even *White-Jacket* are we asked to subscribe to some world-view. This is only a story, a narrative of "what befell" certain men in the year of the Great Mutiny. What does require our option, however, is the manner of the telling, the compassion and patiently exact utterance of the writer who has "sung" the story; for it is through these that we are brought to "believe" in the degree of virtue claimed for its protagonists.

"What one notices in him," E. M. Forster said of the Melville of *Billy Budd*, "is that his apprehensions are free from personal worry." [11] His imagination and compassion work immediately, taking fair and full measure of their impressive objects. This cannot be said of all of Melville's work, in much of which (most damagingly in *Pierre*) all we can clearly see at times are the features of his own discomposure. And given the circumstances of the writing of *Billy Budd*—his career as an author of books thirty years behind him, his life closing down, his own two boys dead and his old energies gone—we might reasonably expect incoherence, failure of control. Instead we find a concentration, and integrity, of performance that match the best in his earlier career. The achievement, and the act of mind it speaks for, are indeed extraordinary. The particulars of this story positively invited misconstruction, as they still invite misinterpretation. Straining after dramatic effect or insistence on an allegorical lesson could only have diminished its grave authority. Mere indignation or pity would have left it no more than a parable of injustice, an exercise in resentment. But there is no indignation or outrage in the telling of *Billy Budd*—no quarrel at all, with God or society or law or nature or any agency of human suffering. Rather there is a poise and sureness of judgment (but at no loss of the appetite for explanation); a compassionate objectivity which, claiming

[11] *Aspects of the Novel*, p. 206.

no credit for itself, keeps its fine temper before the worst appearances; most of all, a readiness of apprehension possible only to an actual, measurable greatness of mind. That is to say, there is intellectual magnanimity—which Milton proposed in his treatise on Christian doctrine as the greatest of that "first class of special virtues connected with the duty of man towards himself."

This is the example the Melville of *Billy Budd* offers as a writer. A personal example, of course, but also a formal example, and of the most radical sort—as Henry James would remind us in declaring that "the deepest quality of a work of art will always be the quality of the mind of the producer." If we add that this quality does not come full-blown into the world but must be made and exercised, like any rational creation, then we may at least imagine how Melville's still barely tapped capacity to "influence" might yet be productively exploited, and his legacy as a writer husbanded and renewed.

CHAPTER NINE

MELVILLE'S EXAMPLE

". . . both to disclose the world and to offer it as a task to the generosity of the reader."—SARTRE, "Why Write?"

". . . above all a man of letters. . . ."—CESARE PAVESE, Introduction to *Moby-Dick* (1932)

"IS NOT STYLE born out of the shock of new material?" —so Yeats remembered and wrote down a remark of Synge's.[1] But the new material of art, of creative performance, does not fall into the writer's lap; neither does it come at his bidding. More probably it hides in the shadow of what is already in plain view. The power to distinguish it, of course, but also the readiness to receive it, the openness to it and equability before it, make all the difference. In Chapter Seven mention was made of certain masterful paragraphs in *Moby-Dick* which are instruments of the narrative's furthest penetration and thus of its greatest originality, yet which as we come upon them appear to be given to us almost accidentally. They seem, at the outset, as casual as afterthoughts. But in their few lines they probe down to an unsuspected deeper core of truth and so become of utmost importance for the book as a whole. It is as if the writer, at the end of some rounded and perfectly efficient passage of major exposition, has found himself—to his surprise perhaps—unready to let go. Something he had not anticipated, which nevertheless appears in the very shape of what he was casting for, may at the last moment have touched

[1] "The Bounty of Sweden," section i.

and slipped his outfloating net, and he must lower again or in all honesty confess a failure. Or an obstacle has come out of hiding—the writer's ordinary skill may conceal it from everyone except himself—and must be got around; a blank is felt, and must be acknowledged. In any event, what now he moves ahead to is not, as he sees it, the mere embellishment or underscoring of what is already well enough expressed. It is rather a continuation of the plain primary work of inquiry and designation, the further possible extent of which the very thoroughness of his own developing effort has been the means of disclosing. The discovery, the style-forging shock of new insight, is self-generated. Similarly, if the result should be some extraordinary additional richness of emphasis and assertion (as is the case with the paragraphs cited from *Moby-Dick*), that in turn is only a by-product of this immediate particular effort of right designation; an effort—as it must have seemed when being carried out—simply after a greater measure of explicitness.

"One is not a writer for having chosen to say certain things," Sartre postulates, "but for having chosen to say them in a certain way." It is the way of Melville's saying that I have been concerned with throughout this book. The authority his name and work still have for us testifies, of course, to the gravity of his themes and the amplitude of his address to them, yet the virtue that finally holds us to him as a writer is specifically a literary virtue. It is an exertion of mastery over certain elected forms of prose narration. So the leading question for criticism is not, what did Melville think, or, what system of understanding can be assembled from his successive books (matters, after all, of plain record; we need only to read him carefully), but rather, what is the nature of the example he presents of the work of imaginative creation, and of that process of free conversion by which thought, feeling, observation, fact, judgment, vision, are fixed into the abiding forms of his art.

More simply: within the chosen directions of his work, what virtue shows itself and works itself out? With Melville, it is this exceptional persistence and tenacity in imaginative definition that seems to me the distinguishing thing. He goes on to the end of what (he happens to discover) can be shown and said; he completes the figure. This is not the same as pursuing an effort to round out ideas or perfect orderly structures of argument. Conceptual thoroughness, methodical inquiry and tabulation, are not in his line (though in the encyclopedic mass of *Moby-Dick* he brilliantly mimes the fashion of such writing, and incidentally suggests what its true goal should be). Melville was not in any proper sense a thinker; and in this book it has not seemed to me in the nature of the work he actually undertook to extract from it a structure of thought, of ideas, even of themes and summary images. We can see quickly enough that he stands squarely in that central tradition of American writing which combines the confession of personal experience with the high vocation of truth-divining and witness-bearing. But we see also that Melville's working imagination is of that type which Santayana defined as typically American-pragmatic—a type which, as it seems, hardly distinguishes its artistic intention from the "potency" it comes to feel in itself and in the things that excite it, and which therefore characteristically delivers itself in "premonitions and prophecies." [2] Such an imagination is not necessarily indifferent to conventional forms of exposition—and without the generous conventions of the narrated story Melville's achievement is inconceivable. But it treats them cavalierly, as merest conveniences. It abides by them, it as easily breaks them; it uses them as channels to flow in, or to overflow; it hardly notices their assistance. In the process it will run extreme risks of confusion and incoherence—but finds its justification in thereby the more directly and plentifully releasing the priceless free power of original insight.

What I think most impressive in Melville is just this plenitude of released and extended power, acting to realize itself in a sufficient language through all the turns of his exposition.

[2] "Materialism and Idealism in American Life," in *Character and Opinion in the United States* (New York, 1920).

Now to make the case for an author in these terms, rather than as a definer of truths or projector of universal forms and meanings, may appear, from some points of view, to diminish his importance in the scale of general value. To my mind, however, it shows him the more significant artist. It reveals as no listing of great themes could ever do the unique force of his example. For what is art if not power seeking the justification (not to say benediction) of incomparable form? It is the peculiarity of created objects that chiefly compels attention—but also, and not less, the directed energy that (we gradually realize) must have been at work to enable them to develop and hold their inimitable fashioning. At this level our vision of them has to be double. We can imagine some other object, some other form or meaning, but not some other effect. Some such understanding, I think, is at the core of Pasternak's magisterial definition (which eloquently confirms and particularizes the point of view I am trying to state) of all greatly expressive art, and what is exemplary in it: that it is "more one-sided than people think"; that it is above all else "the symbol of power"; that in recording the metaphor-creating "displacements" of natural reality worked by spirit and feeling, it always makes power its deeper theme, whatever the sponsoring occasion, and is born in the realization of that theme; but that it expresses the theme of power (which cannot express itself unaided) in the language that is peculiarly art's own—"the two-fold language of images, that is, the language of accompanying features." [3]

By this measure the *first* test of art is the consummation of particular images and features. They only need not to be taken as ends in themselves. They are created phenomena, and never wholly cease to represent the pleasure of their creator. Their reality in any case is virtual. To practical criticism the scale and volume do not immediately matter, except as an indication of probable difficulties. As for the question of truth and of

[3] *Safe Conduct*, I, vii, tr. Beatrice Scott. Similarly: "The clearest, most memorable and important fact about art is its conception, and the world's best creations, those which tell of the most diverse things, in reality describe their own birth."

relevance—more than anyone but the maker himself can quite believe, the languages he works in (as here defined: the languages of image and feature as well as of style and form) impose a sufficient discipline, and hold him to reality. What is unforgivable is simply any slacking off, any deliberate withholding, of the imaginative attack and of the pursuit of words to consolidate its advances. So I should argue once more that the decisive immediate virtue in Melville's prose is the insistent thrust forward it develops toward an entire explicitness, an unstinting exactness. This virtue, as we find it, is not limited to special operations like encyclopedic description or the analysis of character. Rather it is generic and constitutional. It marks his simplest rendering of physical objects and actions; it equally animates the moral and psychological probings of his most strenuously ambitious work. After a thirty-year interval it is as strong as ever in *Billy Budd*, though much else has gone by the board. Scarcely a sentence in Melville's best writing is not stamped with its urgency: an odd adjective; a defining participle; an unexpected sequence of verbs; circuitous and often distracting parentheses; imputations from all points of the compass as to cause and origin, category and probability, special feature and general law—all aimed at discovering the precise and entire mode of existence of the matter at hand. Without this virtue the ingratiating mannerisms of Melville's ordinary style would largely have gone to waste (though it is also a cause of tediousness and overwriting). "Thrust toward explication" might be more exact: he will lay it all open and he will get it all said. Like so many of the major Americans he is an explainer, and his narratives are often most satisfactory (contrary to textbook dogmas) when most directly explanatory. His art, not always under control, is in keeping this will-to-explain in the service of his prime narrative objects—their definition, their clarification.

And what he was moved to say of them he did find the words for—with a thoroughness and consistency, I think, that are matched by no other of our prose masters except the undistractible Emerson. This seems to me the prime truth about Melville as a writer. So in inquiring into the meaning of this or that story we may fairly assume that he has tried to say it out as best he can. The explanations he advances are not usually simple, but they are not short-circuited or evasive, and they are not obscure; he summons the energy, the patience, to carry them through to an end. In this effort, of course, his natural instinct for the specific capacities of the words, idioms, and rhythms of written English is indispensable to him. Equally important, and at the heart of Melville's power to persuade, is the sureness of his feeling for what is needed at any given point by way of presentation and explanation (very different from his damaging uncertainty in, say, *Pierre* as to what exactly it was that he wanted to present and explain). That kind of expressive tact is not in itself inordinately remarkable in literature. The astonishing thing in Melville is its conjunction with great power, with extraordinary purposefulness, with an imagination whose intense grasp was not likely ever to be wholly appeased at any stage of its encounter with life.

To come into the presence of such a writer is to experience a broadening of apprehension and—perhaps even more important—a positive strengthening of capability. We are tempted indeed to live in his work vicariously. We attribute every kind of significance to it, or make a cult of it and become its apostles—and in so doing risk losing sight of its actual nature as art or work, its untranslatable particularity.[4] We need to

[4] The risk we ourselves run in this is not inconsiderable. So the young Emerson understood in noting, at twenty, the ambiguity of his own exaltation over the famous passage of self-dedication in the second book of Milton's *Reason of Church Government*. Such reactions, he told himself, can warm the soul "to the love of virtue and greatness" and are therefore precious, but they can also "leave one fruit that may be poisonous: they leave a self-complacency arising from having thought so nobly for a moment, which leads the self-deceiver to believe himself better than other men." The general danger is even greater. It is the danger that fervent minds, so acted upon and reacting, will be led into "a *poetical* religion," arising from all "the tendencies of the age"—thus Emerson in 1823,

remind ourselves again and again, astonished by the example of performance it offers, what it really is: in the case of Melville a body of freely reflective prose narration brought into being by a mind that found its opportunity in the telling of stories, the recording in so many words of certain actual men and events.

That is to say, by one who, within his own distinctive practice, was "above all a man of letters." Pavese's emphasis, of thirty years ago, seems to me the right one still. The general conditions of culture and communication have changed radically in our era and are still changing, in such a way that we find it increasingly hard to imagine how any one book or author or specimen of creative performance can make a difference in the relentless unfolding of life and fortune. But writing itself—the whole wide impersonal vocation of letters, the consuming service to words and expressive forms, the resolute transposition of experience into figures of statement that are both communicable and complete—makes an extraordinary difference. And the writers who matter are those whose service has kept this vocation, and the powers of mind it requires, tensile and alive. This is the point, I think, of Pavese's judgment. "Reading Melville, who was not ashamed to begin *Moby-Dick* . . . with eight pages of quotations and to go on by discussing, quoting again, and being the man of letters, you expand your lungs, you enlarge your brain, you feel alive and more of a man." And the greatness of the book as a whole is that once begun in this way, it does not let you down: from start to finish the "serenity and clarity" of the directing voice are such that for all the darkness of the action "you leave the theatre each time with a sense of increased vitality." [5]

---

nearly fifty years before *Culture and Anarchy*, and more than a hundred in advance of *Science and Poetry*.

[5] Cesare Pavese, "The Literary Whaler," *Sewanee Review*, LXVIII (Summer 1960), 407–418, trans. B. M. Arnett. Pavese's essay, written at twenty-five and in the depths of the Fascist repression, seems to me one of the few indispensable contributions of criticism to a just appreciation of *Moby-Dick*. (Has anyone else seen so well the virtue of those opening "Extracts"?)

Of the possibilities of action in life, men speak to us after their kind, out of the chances that fall to them. Ideologues harangue us, converters attempt to convert us, analysts analyze us (and explain away the analysis we learn to make of them), good citizens tell us what the good really is, custodians of value instruct us in value-ratings, appointed guardians stand firm against the accidental and naïve on behalf of "maturity" and "responsibility"—but what all these spokesmen see, or tell us that they see, and what we in like manner tell ourselves, is never quite the same as what our unguarded instinct (fantastically educated, whether we like it or not) gives us its incessant signals of. Impatient to lay hands on the axis of reality, they tighten their grip too soon. Anxious to produce effects, they produce half-effects—than which there is no commodity more likely to spoil, and perhaps more deadly. In short, they are negligent of their words, and it is their words that first and always betray them. A Melville, on the other hand, a mere writer, devoting himself without constraint (whatever else he has in mind) to the forming of his work and to a corresponding mastery of letters, rarely causes as much to happen as they do; he only outlives them. And that is the great virtue of his example, morally speaking. That is his unique and irreplaceable contribution—to have made so brave a show of renewing the lost opportunities of that life which, however often it defeats us and however finally, is the one life we are given, and which still (by a reciprocal charity it would take a life's work even to learn the extent of) remains somehow to be made.

INDEX